RAMONES

THE COMPLETE TWISTED HISTORY

Dick Porter

T0151135

Plexus, London

British Library Cataloguing in Publication Data

Porter, Dick
  Ramones : a complete twisted history
  1.Ramones (Musical group) 2. Punk rock musicians - United
  States - Biography 3. Rock groups - United States - Biography
  I.Title
  782.4'2166'0922

ISBN 0 85965 326 9

Cover design by Phil Smee, Phil Gambrill and Brian Flynn
Book design by Brian Flynn
Printed and bound in Spain by Bookprint, S.L., Barcelona

Contents

cracked the American charts with the single 'Saturday Night', the chorus of which provided inspiration for the 'Hey, ho! Lets go!' refrain of 'Blitzkrieg Bop'.

At the height of the progressive rock era, the Ramones were keeping things short and to the point, writing songs about sniffing glue or beating up brats. As Joey recalls, the band saw themselves as excluded from normality: 'We couldn't write about love or cars, so we sang about this stuff, like glue sniffing. We thought it was funny.' Such crude simplicity was enhanced by velocity. Like most bands, the group would be significantly faster live than on vinyl. But the Ramones took this to extremes – often completing a set of fifteen songs in around eighteen minutes. Throughout their 22-year existence, they would only once record a song that ran for longer than four and a half minutes. The simple blitzkrieg assault of the Ramones instantly threw the musical soundscape of the mid-Seventies into sharp definition.

The band debuted as a trio: Doug (Dee Dee Ramone) Colvin on bass and vocals, John (Johnny Ramone) Cummings on guitar, and Jeffrey (Joey Ramone) Hyman on drums. The adoption of a common surname indicated how they wanted to be viewed collectively – they also dressed similarly, and initially shared all writing credits.

I think rock 'n' roll should be three words and a chorus, and the three words should be good enough to say it all. *Dee Dee Ramone*

The name 'Ramones' was selected from a list of possibles on the basis that it sounded like a gang name. Originally a pseudonym adopted by Paul McCartney, it was the name he used to book into hotels with the Beatles to ensure a minimum of public and press intrusion.

The style and sound of the newly baptised group were notable for their absolute lack of pretension. 'We are as we seem,' insisted Joey. Irrespective of their glam-rock influences, the band simply took the stage in the same clothes they walked around in. In fact, there was never any grand design in place – the Ramones were simply a neighbourhood band. 'I knew John from seeing him around and hanging out after high school,' recalled Joey. 'He and Tommy were friends and he was in a band with my brother. Then I got to be friends with Dee Dee, and he and John were friends too. He mentioned me to John and John called and asked me to be in a band.' The motivation behind Johnny's call was simple: he had been laid off from his construction job, and decided to try music as an alternative means of earning a living.

Jeffrey Hyman was born in the middle-class, primarily Jewish neighbourhood of Forest Hills, Queens on 19 May 1951. Despite enjoying a relatively affluent childhood, the future Joey Ramone struggled to come to terms with the divorce of his parents when he

Joey Ramone – ripped and torn, 1976.

was eight years old. His father, Noel Hyman, was the boss of a Manhattan-based trucking company. In common with many small businessmen in the borough, Hyman had an abrasive nature that manifested in a domineering attitude toward his wife, Charlotte, and his son. Arguments were not uncommon in the Hyman household, and Joey took refuge in music and television. His discovery of pop radio opened up an avenue of escapism – as he later recalled, 'Music was my salvation – the transistor radio, listening to WMCA Good Guys and Murray the K.'

As a child, Joey was somewhat withdrawn and made little impression at school. As he later observed, 'there's a lot of people that really get into being in high school; they go to dances and all that shit. I always hated those people.' Aside from music, he had little in the way of hobbies and, like most kids born after 1950, spent much of his spare time watching TV.

Although he was the recipient of some mild bullying caused by his gangling, dishevelled appearance, he was strong-willed and soon adopted the long hair and distressed denim of the adolescent rebel. Following an initial dalliance with the accordion, Joey fixed his sights on playing the drums. He soon began to construct a rudimentary kit, partly financed by King Korn supermarket trading stamps.

When we started out, we were alone, basically because nobody sounded like us. And it was always difficult. You're always alone. *Joey Ramone*

'I tried to get him interested in some good music,' Noel Hyman explained, 'his grandmother, Fanny, used to sing for Macy's; you rented a piano from the store for a party and she came with it – so I got him an accordion when he was a child. He loved the goddamn thing, but he squeezed it until there was nothing left of it – I think he loved to hear the wheezy noise it made. As a teenager he was fairly good at the drums, playing 'em in the basement with his friends, but it got so I really had a hard time standing the racket.'

Following her divorce from Noel, Joey's mother, Charlotte Lesher, continued bringing up Joey and his younger brother, Mickey Leigh, while running a gallery called the Art Garden on Queens Boulevard. In spite of her busy lifestyle, Charlotte found time to be supportive of his (and brother Mickey's) musical ambitions. 'They loved the music,' she testified, 'especially when the Beatles came to New York . . . I wanted them to have some interests and they wanted music lessons. Mickey wanted the guitar and Joey wanted the drums. So I got them lessons, and from that moment on music was a very important part of their lives.'

At the age of thirteen, Joey's grandmother bought him a drum kit, which he took to with brio, emulating the demented style of his heroes, Keith Moon and Ginger Baker. The two brothers held regular practice sessions in the basement of their home, and the small space soon became a hang-out for neighbourhood friends.

In Charlotte, Joey and Mickey were blessed with a particularly groovy parent, who tolerated their constant din and reacted in an enlightened manner when she became aware of teenage pot smoking. Charlotte preferred her kids to conduct their narcotic experiments indoors, as she 'didn't want them to do it outside where they could be busted.'

She also encouraged Joey's earliest attempts at song writing. 'Joey started writing songs on scraps of paper and the backs of shopping bags,' she later recalled. 'Really weird songs, and he'd say, "Listen to this ma. Tell me what you think of this," and I'd say, "Well, that's very good. I like that." The idea was to always be encouraging and supportive. And the damn thing is, after a while, I really began to like them. I thought they were very good. Ever since they were very young and they both had groups, I've been going and dragging other people to their shows.'

In spite of being the only Ramone actually born in Forest Hills, Joey had no sense of attachment to the suburbs and was keen to escape his surroundings. As Charlotte later recalled, 'Forest Hills is a very conservative, conventional place. I think we were the black-sheep household of our street.'

After leaving high school against his mother's wishes, Joey began hanging out in Greenwich Village where he raised cash by distributing flyers for massage parlours and selling plastic flowers. 'My brother was a real hippie in those days,' explains Mickey Leigh. 'He used to walk around with no shoes on, and he went to San Francisco, and he hung out with hippies.'

During this period Joey auditioned for hippie rocker James Barry Keefer, who had scored minor hits ('98.6', 'Ain't Gonna Lie', 'Tell Me To My Face' and 'Daylight Savin' Time') under the name of 'Keith'. 'I auditioned for him, playing drums. He took me out for a beer and it was exciting, y'know? When I first got to his loft he was blow-drying his hair. I brought my double bass Keith Moon set of drums up there. But he was fucked up because he made me play in a room all by myself, without accompanying me, or anything. He said, "Alright – play!" So I played "Toad" or something, y'know? The fuckin' jerk!'

Following a brief spell in a mental ward caused by some bad acid, and an arrest for unlawfully peddling plastic flowers, Joey abandoned his soap-dodging lifestyle. 'Joey was such a mess that my mother threw him out,' recalled Mickey. 'She was going out with this guy, Phil, who later became a psychologist . . . Phil was the one who suggested that Joey leave the house, because Joey was like twenty, 21 and he wasn't doing anything. And it didn't seem like he was going to do anything.'

Joey's mother provided him with steady employment at the Art Garden, which he often used as a crash pad, arranging the paintings to screen him from passing police cars at night. While he adapted to the role of modern art salesman and was accepted by the predominantly retired, Jewish clientele, Joey's fascination with music remained unabated. Ultimately he quit, signing on for welfare to fully concentrate on his latest project, a glam rock band called Sniper.

He also became a regular at gigs on the local circuit, catching the New York Dolls and the Dictators. Adopting the space-race/glam-style name of Jeff Starship, Joey began to develop his unique vocal style, a Queens-crossed-with-Dick-Van-Dyke-'mockney' annunciation, his sour NY accent merging with the mock-British element to produce a diction verging on parody. As Tommy later observed, 'Joey sang with a cockney accent because he loved English bands like Herman's Hermits. The funny thing is, when English groups like the Clash started, they all sang with cockney accents. Joey from Queens initiated cockney singing in punk rock!' (The best illustration of Joey's affected vocals appears on the demo version of 'I Don't Care', which the Ramones would record in late 1974 – found on the excellent remastered CD of *Ramones*, issued by Warner Archives/Rhino in 2001.)

Joey described Sniper, who played regular local gigs, as 'a glitter band with a lot of attitude . . . I liked getting dressed up and my look still wasn't the one of Ramones,' he lated recalled. 'I wore pink boots, a black silk shirt, leather gloves up to the elbow, black glasses and long hair. It was very exciting and in those days you could do it, although a lot of people wanted to kill me.'

It was at one of these shows that Joey first encountered Dee Dee, who recalls, 'I think I wanted to get Joey in the band. I saw him do a gig as the lead singer of another band, and I said, y'know, I want this guy, he's unique. He was the first singer I'd seen who wasn't copying Mick Jagger.' Before long, Dee Dee was crashing on the floor of the Art Garden. 'No furniture, no nothing. It was just a paint store and we slept on the floor in the stock room,' he recalled. 'Joey was painting then. He would chop up carrots and lettuce and turnips and strawberries and mix it all together and paint with them. His paintings were very good.'

'I knew Johnny from seeing him after school,' explained Joey. 'Tommy and he were friends and he played in a band with my brother Mitch [Mickey Leigh]. In the meantime I became friends with Dee Dee, who was already a friend of Johnny's and after a meeting between the two of them they asked to become a member of the group. I was very happy and I thought that Johnny and Dee Dee were very cool and had a very cool look too although torn jeans, leather jacket and sneakers was what they wore every day. We are what we look like.'

Reflecting upon their early influences, Joey explained, 'We were inspired by a lot of different things. It was getting out your frustrations and your aggressions, writing things that we were dissatisfied with like the state of the radio, things that we found amusing – TV and movies. Horror movies, "B" films and stuff. Like the song "I Don't Wanna Go Down To The Basement".'

More particularly, Joey cited Detroit revolutionaries the MC5 and Wolverhampton yob-rockers Slade as of particular significance on account of their emphasis on simplicity and energy, as opposed to complexity: 'They made us realise, that we didn't have to write *songs* to be a band.' Coincidentally, Joey later received lessons in breathing technique from the same voice coach who had taught Slade's Noddy Holder.

Joey's angular, 6' 3"-physique and long lank black hair lent him a certain visual distinction. He moved little on stage, forming a tripod with the mike stand to deliver his vocal, with a deadpan menace that owed something to Alice Cooper. 'I liked the whole theatrical glitter thing he was doing and that he was very primal, like Iggy and the Stooges,' he recalled.

Like the rest of the Ramones, Joey was always a fan of the Stooges – a relentless noise machine with little interest in the 'peace and love' zeitgeist of the late 1960s, concentrating on a bleakly hedonistic approach to sex, drugs and rock 'n' roll. Fronted by the charismatic Iggy Pop (born James Osterberg), they stripped rock 'n' roll down to its barest components in much the same way the Ramones would do later. This reductive approach left observers little to focus on save for the group's sonic assault and Iggy's bravura onstage antics. Live, the band rarely disappointed, and although the sight of a shirtless Iggy – caked in blood or peanut butter, rolling around on a stage strewn with broken glass – offended the sensibilities of the flower children, the Stooges soon gained a hardcore following.

Elektra 'company freak' Danny Fields quickly assumed management of the band, and the Stooges' self-titled debut album was produced by John Cale, formerly of the Velvet Underground. *The Stooges* was described by Fields as 'twenty years ahead of its time', despite critical acclaim and tracks such as '1969', 'I Wanna Be Your Dog' and 'No Fun' (all later cited as punk classics), *The Stooges* failed to sell. Iggy's love of substance abuse meant he often had to be revived from near-unconsciousness before gigs, and, following the band's second commercially unsuccessful album, *Fun House*, he withdrew into heroin addiction as the Stooges effectively fell apart. James Williamson joined as lead guitarist, but, with a similar chemical outlook to Iggy, he hardly helped to stabilise matters. Occasional attempts at recording demos were made, but the Stooges spent the best part of two years in creative limbo.

Hope of a revival arrived in the metamorphic shape of David Bowie. Inspired by their atonal assault, he coaxed the Stooges into the studio to record a third album. *Raw Power* was released in 1973, and, while it was a further sales disaster that led to the band's demise, it would ultimately be recognised as the sonic template for the punk canon. Bowie's production had a brittle quality later replicated by the Ramones and the Dead Boys.

Describing the Stooges' influence on punk, Iggy asserts, 'Musically we never played one track that adheres to the standard punk approach. But we had an attitude, and it was the things we sang about and that we dared to be simple about it . . . The first pogoing, stage diving, snarling use of the word "destroy" and the word "punk" in reference to us, that all started with us. And the Ramones dressed exactly like I used to dress, but did their own thing musically.' Although critical of Iggy Pop's later direction, Joey would compliment the chemistry between James Williamson and Iggy as 'the perfect combination'.

But it was also Joey who was responsible for much of the 'bubblegum' aspect of the Ramones' sound. 'I wrote "Beat on the Brat" about the spoiled brats in Queens,' he revealed. 'That chord change at the top of the song

Iggy Pop, with the Stooges – 'We had an attitude.'

comes directly from those bubblegum songs – "Chewy, Chewy", "Yummy, Yummy, Yummy" . . . all those fun songs.'

Born on 8 October 1948, John Cummings was the only son of a Long Island builder. John was an active and healthy child, and soon began to develop a lifelong obsession with baseball. A gifted athlete, he attracted the attention of his high school coach. However, irrespective of his love for the game, the code of discipline associated with sports ran contrary to Johnny's youthful nature and he swiftly shifted his focus to pop music.

Initially inspired by the raw rock 'n' roll of early Presley, he bought a guitar but was discouraged by his inability to emulate the likes of Jimi Hendrix and Jimmy Page. Despite this, his tastes broadened to include late Fifties icons such as Buddy Holly, Gene Pitney, Chuck Berry and Dion. His interest in becoming a musician resurfaced after meeting up with Tommy Erdelyi in the high school canteen.

Tommy and Johnny then joined a local band, the Tangerine Puppets, as bassist and guitarist respectively. The Puppets were a garage band influenced by the primal blues-rock of Bo Diddley and the tremolo-laden surf sound of Dick Dale. Johnny's guitar influences also included Jimi Hendrix and the MC5's Fred 'Sonic' Smith. Like Joey and Dee Dee, Johnny was also an admirer of Slade and the New York Dolls. 'When I saw the New York Dolls and Slade in 1972/73, what I saw were two bands that were really entertaining. I saw limitations but they had songs, power and image. It made me feel like I could go get a guitar, that I can do this too. Which is what kids felt when they saw the Ramones.'

Johnny's admiration of Fred Smith's distinctive sound influenced his choice of guitar, when he purchased a blue Mosrite, similar to that used by Smith, for $50 in January 1974. In keeping with the reputation he would later acquire for thrift, Johnny selected the Mosrite 'because it was the cheapest guitar in the store'.

On leaving school, 'I went to college because of the Vietnam war,' explains Johnny, 'but I had a high draft number so it was very unlikely anyway. Every eligible kid in the country was ahead of me. I was against it. It wasn't a good war like World War II.'

Dee Dee would later lampoon the Ramones' call-up for the draft to provide outrageous copy: 'We said we wanted to go and kill some Chinks, but the Army thought we must be mad. They would only take people who didn't want to go.' Joey also made his own contribution: 'I tried to join up, but they ah uhh, said I'd have to kill geeks . . . uh, gooks.'

After dropping out, Johnny drifted through a number of menial jobs and periods on welfare, before eventually following his father into the construction industry. It was while working on a site on Broadway that he first began hanging out with Dee Dee, enduring a brief stint as a mail clerk in an adjacent office. 'John is a very strong willed person. He was one of the first friends I made when I moved to America,' alienated forces brat Dee Dee later confided, 'and our friendship was based on music. When I first told John that the Stooges were my favourite group, he said he liked them also. Someone else in Forest Hills liked the Stooges besides me. It was like a miracle.' Johnny added, 'While we sat out eating and watching the girls pass by, we decided to start a group.'

Mean, moody and magnificent – Johnny shows his Mosrite who's boss, 1976.

Johnny and Joey live at CBGB's, 1977.

Wanna Be Someone

They are very, very nice boys
Charlotte Lesher

Once accustomed to his newly-purchased axe, Johnny boiled down the sum of his influences to an essence with no identifying elements: 'Pure, white rock 'n' roll, with no blues influence. I wanted our sound to be as original as possible,' he recalls.

This concept of 'pure white rock 'n' roll' is oxymoronic, given that the whole genre was derived from black musicians. However, as a reaction against the prevailing hippie aesthetic, Johnny's logic becomes clear. 'In the Sixties hippies always wanted to be black,' explains Legs McNeil. 'We were going: "Fuck the blues, fuck the black experience." We had nothing in common with black people at that time – we'd had ten years of being politically correct and we were going to have fun, like kids are supposed to do.'

Johnny's guitar technique was one of reductive simplicity, eschewing solos and concentrating on the most basic barre chords. 'He created everything with his down-picking, his strum,' recalled Joey. 'In sound checks the band would do a couple of songs without vocals. I'd listen to Johnny's guitar and hear all these harmonics, these instruments like organ and piano that weren't really there. And he didn't use any effects.'

Visually, Johnny's style was eye-catching. He would stand, unsmiling and motionless, his legs spread apart with the guitar slung as low as possible, playing only downstrokes from the wrist with such ferocity that a thin spray of blood from his fingertips splattered the scratch plate. Dee Dee would mirror Johnny, and the two guitarists appeared like grim bookends on either side of the serpentine Joey.

Johnny was the driving force. While Tommy would provide the technical know-how and the industry connections to ensure the band got heard, Johnny's authoritarian nature ensured the Ramones always attended rehearsals on time.

He was also fiercely patriotic, and had a teenage fascination with the armed forces Despite his initial misgivings, he would later revise his attitude toward Vietnam in favour of a more hawkish stance: 'I wanted to be a soldier. So did Dee Dee. I wanted to go to military school, the battlefield, 'Nam.'

Johnny had a stable upbringing, with such a degree of parental control that he was reluctant to tell his mother and father he'd become a Ramone. But he wasn't averse to a spot of misbehaviour – he turned up at the Beatles' 1966 Shea Stadium concert with a bag of rocks 'as big as baseballs' that he hurled at the band with relish. As Johnny later attested, 'we lived right near the park [where Shea Stadium is located]. Yeah, we saw all the rock concerts there . . . we used to be vandals. We used to rip the TV's off the roof [of Johnny's block], though, throw 'em down into the street . . . used to go round and throw rocks, bottles through people's windows.'

Warming to life as a 'general nogoodnick', Johnny next tried his hand at breaking and entering. 'It was in a whole row of stores and we broke into the laundromat from behind by mistake,' he told *Rolling Stone*. 'The next time we tried robbing a bakery on 63rd Drive; somebody climbed in the window above the door. The police came to my house the next day and asked somebody to identify me, but the person said I wasn't the

The only time I say I'm a musician is when I have to fill out the tax forms, but I don't feel comfortable with it. I don't have any guitar at home, I have never improved since I started playing and I don't want to do. I always thought that he who changes, changes for the worst; only the Beatles changed with success from album to album. If Elvis wouldn't have changed he would have been very effective. *Johnny Ramone*

one. The other kid finked on me – but I don't care 'cause he's gotten killed since then.'

Ultimately, Johnny experienced a kind of epiphany and decided he was wasting his time as a local thug. 'One day, suddenly, a voice from above: what am I doing with my life? Is this what I'm here for, to be a delinquent? So I quit everything I had been doing wrong: stop with alcohol, drugs and every other excess, from then on the only password was "self discipline".'

Douglas Glen Colvin, aka Dee Dee, was born on 18 September 1952, into a military environment. His father was an army officer who had fought at the Battle of the Bulge. Colvin Snr's postings took the family away from Dee Dee's Fort Lee, Virginia birthplace to Tokyo, Massachusetts and Munich. The austere post-war surroundings of Munich left a profound impression on him. He grew up playing on bombsites, and would later allude to Germany, fascism and military themes in his lyrics.

As with Joey, Dee Dee's home environment was fraught with turbulence. He described his mother as 'a drunken nut job', and his father as a violent man who beat his wife and son. Dee Dee's father had married a German girl some seventeen years his

A well scrubbed Dee Dee in Amsterdam, May 1977.

The Ramones spell it out. (Joey, Dee Dee, Johnny, Tommy).

junior, while stationed in Berlin after the Korean War. He was a hard-nosed master sergeant who liked to hang out with his army buddies, while his mother, although traumatised by the effects of growing up under Hitler during World War II, was more of a free spirit. The family unit remained together until Dee Dee was fifteen, when his parents' differences were accelerated by regular drunken arguments.

Dee Dee's introduction to rock 'n' roll came courtesy of his mother, who was a fan of Bill Haley and Elvis Presley. The new music left a profound impression, and he was equally struck by the way rockers dressed. 'You couldn't ignore the teenagers in pegged black chinos and greasy hairdos,' he recalled, 'boppin' around the Munich American High School, which was right near the building where I lived.'

The family briefly returned to the US, when Sgt. Colvin was stationed in Atlanta, Georgia during the Cuban Missile Crisis. Dee Dee recalls being utterly miserable, even contemplating suicide, during this period. His European background left him isolated from his high school classmates. He started sniffing glue, the first in a line of habits that would culminate in full-blown smack addiction, and eventually precipitate his death.

His parents' relationship continued to deteriorate, as his father embarked on a succession of affairs. But Dee Dee's misery was relieved by an immersion in rock 'n' roll, comic books and monster movies. He was a fixture at the local picture-house and, at weekends, often attended dances at the local army base with his mother and younger sister, Beverly.

The next stop on the Colvin family world tour was the German industrial town of Pirmasens, which Dee Dee described as 'a violent, anything-goes kind of place'. Constant relocation meant Dee Dee had little opportunity to establish friendships, and had become something of a loner. 'I didn't have many friends,' he later recalled. 'I never have.'

He filled this void with music and drugs. The discovery of some tubes of liquid morphine hidden in a garbage dump served as an introduction to opiates; despite much of his initial find being confiscated by his father. Subsequent exposure to Radio Luxembourg and a doomed attempt to master the guitar provided Dee Dee with less harmful kicks. He became a fan of the Beatles, adopting the mop-top hairstyle and purchasing a Beatle suit to go with it.

His penchant for discovering discarded things also led to a pile of *Playboy* magazines, wherein he noticed an article about a wrestler named Gorgeous George. Possibly due to his own unhappiness, the idea of creating an alter ego struck a chord with young Colvin, and, for reasons he could never really explain, he decided to adopt the name 'Dee Dee'. As he observed in his autobiography, *Lobotomy: Surviving the Ramones*, 'It was in style then, and John Lennon called himself Johnny Silver. George [Harrison] was George Perkins and Paul [McCartney] was Paul Ramone. I thought it was pretty outrageous to change your name to a made up one, but I liked the idea. I was lost in another fantasy, and changed from Douglas Colvin to Dee Dee Ramone.'

We didn't receive proper guidance from our parents.

Dee Dee Ramone

Becoming aware of the Berlin music scene, Dee Dee began taking in local bands who performed cover versions of the current hits. Unsurprisingly, it was the big names from the US and Britain who made the bigger impact. 'It was a great time for music,' he recalls. 'I saw the Troggs, the Kinks, the Small Faces, the Hollies, the Beach Boys, the Rolling Stones, the Who and the Walker Brothers.' Reflecting on these influences, Dee Dee later observed, 'Mick Jones and Joe Strummer of the Clash and Steve Jones of the Sex Pistols and I all listened to the same 25 long forgotten songs. Songs like "Sha La La La Lee" by the Small Faces.'

The concerts offered Dee Dee an escape from the isolation of home, where there was usually nobody there – his father was at base, while his mother was usually accompanying his sister to her ballet studies. As a girl, Dee Dee's mother had dreamed of becoming a ballerina, and she was vicariously living out those dreams through her daughter. To extend Beverly's training, Mrs Colvin succeeded in getting her accepted to study at the noted American dance academy, Julliard. It provided a ready-made escape route and they returned to America in 1968, leaving Colvin Snr stationed in Germany.

Dee Dee, Beverly and their mother settled in Forest Hills. Like Joey, Dee Dee found the neighbourhood too mundane and suburban for his tastes. 'Having left my father, I thought things would get better, but they just got stranger. Somehow, I just couldn't relate to my new neighbourhood,' he recalled.

A rift opened up between his mother and sister when Beverly dropped her studies to get married. Not wishing to get embroiled in more domestic bickering, Dee Dee began travelling to nearby Lefrak City, where he'd hang out and get loaded on glue and barbiturates. Venturing further afield, he visited the Greenwich Village clubs he'd read about while in Germany. It led to an expansion of both his musical influences and his consciousness. His mother's reaction to his first experiments with acid was to insist he listen to Hendrix's *Are You Experienced*.

'LSD was fun,' declared Dee Dee. 'I did it hundreds of times and I don't think I ever had any bad trips, but it really wasn't my thing. It was heroin that would get me through the day.' He began drifting into the life of a street punk, hustling for drugs, getting involved with gangs and petty robberies, even engaging in prostitution when cash was short.

If I got angry with someone, I would go for the throat. I thought that was normal. Why do you think I ended up in the Ramones? *Dee Dee Ramone*

In *Please Kill Me*, Legs McNeil and Gillian McCain's oral document of the New York punk scene, Mickey Leigh recounts his reaction to spotting Dee Dee touting for tricks: 'I remember driving by 53rd Street and Third Avenue and seeing Dee Dee Ramone standing out there. He had a black leather motorcycle jacket on, the one he would later wear on the first album cover. He was just standing there, so I knew what he was doing, because I knew that was the gay-boy hustler spot. Still, I was kind of shocked to see somebody I knew standing there, like, "Holy shit! That's Doug standing there. He's really doing it."'

When not hustling to finance his growing smack habit, Dee Dee also worked as an occasional hairdresser and mailroom clerk. It was during this period that he became a face on the New York club scene, regularly attending gigs at clubs such as the Sanctuary, Tamberlane and Superstar.

While enjoying what he described as a 'Harvey Wallbanger and Quaalude' environment, Dee Dee was exposed to the Stooges (who he first saw in 1971), the New York Dolls and the Dictators. 'In the early Seventies rock 'n' roll was like America and Yes – and I hated it,' he explained. 'That's when I started getting into the New York Dolls. Then I discovered the Stooges and that all seemed to go together and the Stooges became my ultimate favourite group. I would just die to go to see them, but they only came to New York every nine months or so. But anytime they ever played New York, I'd see them.'

Dee Dee subsequently tried to start his own band, Satyricon. 'It was a complete disaster. These kids thought I could be a leader. It was one thing having fun in my apartment with little amps, but once we got into a rehearsal studio everything just fell apart.'

Da Brudders at large in Amsterdam, May 1977.

Answering an advertisement in *Andy Warhol's Inter/View* magazine, he unsuccessfully auditioned for the Neon Boys: the band formed by poet/musicians Tom Verlaine and Richard Hell, later to evolve into art-punk pioneers Television.

At this time, Dee Dee was living in an apartment complex adjacent to Johnny and Joey. He recalls hanging out with Joey and getting loaded. 'I had to have different guys to hang out with to do my different drugs with, so I started hanging out with Joey because he liked to drink. But Joey couldn't do drugs. He tried them and he couldn't handle them. He would freak out. One time I saw him smoke some pot and start convulsing on the floor in a foetal position, saying, "I'm freaking out! I'm freaking out!"'

Once Johnny had decided to form a band, Dee Dee accompanied him to Manny's Guitar Centre on 48th Street, selecting a DanElectro bass while Johnny was scoring his Mosrite. Although neither Ramone had any degree of virtuosity, Johnny had some experience with his chosen instrument whereas Dee Dee was a complete novice. 'I had no idea how to tune or play a bass,' he confessed. 'Eventually Johnny would show me the bass parts to my own songs, because I had absolutely no idea how they went on the bass. All I knew was "E".'

Johnny, Dee Dee and Joey held their first rehearsal four days later. As Johnny later recalled, 'We tried to figure out other people's songs at the first rehearsals, but we couldn't, because we had just started to play, so we decided to write our own.'

From the very beginning, Joey and Dee Dee handled the songwriting. 'Joey wrote the way I wrote,' Dee Dee recounted. 'I don't think he knew anything really about guitar chords, or the verse, chorus and intro. Somehow he just banged out these songs on two strings of a Yamaha acoustic guitar and then Johnny would struggle his best to interpret it.'

Further rehearsals ensued, in Charlotte Lesher's basement and at Tommy Erdelyi's Performance Studio rehearsal rooms, where the band were to play their first concert. Erdelyi had been nagging Johnny to get a band together for some time, and quickly became involved in arranging and recording the Ramones' material. Dee Dee had originally opted to play rhythm guitar with a neighbourhood friend, Richie Stern, handling bass duties. 'He was a very special person,' revealed Dee Dee, 'a very crazy supermarket clerk dope-fiend type. He would play Stooges tapes for us and do Iggy impersonations by the light of the glowing TV set.' But, even by the Ramones' reductive standards, Richie was no musician. He left after one rehearsal to pursue a career in banking, necessitating Dee Dee's transfer to bass guitar.

Even a halfwit would know those three chords. *Dee Dee Ramone*

The Ramones' street-tough look was born with their adoption of black leather jackets and torn faded jeans. It was both indicative of their everyday clothing and owed more than a little to the image of 'the Fonz' – from Dee Dee's favourite TV show, the retro-Fifties comedy *Happy Days*.

The pudding-bowl hairstyles favoured by Dee Dee and Johnny were evocative of the Sixties garage bands featured on the *Nuggets* albums. These were compiled by Lenny Kaye, later to become the guitarist for New York punk poet Patti Smith. Bands such as the Trashmen (from whom both the Ramones and seminal psychobillies the Cramps borrowed 'Surfin' Bird') and the Seeds were direct influences on the Ramones. They produced simple no-frills rock, delivered at some velocity during the era of hippie self-indulgence.

Garage-punk had enjoyed a resurgence during the early Seventies, with the release of the first *Nuggets* album. These unpretentious, under-produced songs, heavy on fuzz guitar and without many of the R'n'B influences favoured by Rolling Stones copyists, helped define a type of rock that the Ramones assimilated into their own distinctive sound. As *Punk* magazine founder John Holstrom attests of the seminal New York punk venue, 'The CBGBs jukebox was almost exclusively 1960s garage music, and it was a big reason people came down there and stayed to hang out. Everyone was also aware of [Jonathan Richman's band] the Modern Lovers and Beserkley Records, which was issuing a lot of garage-type music, and

They Don't Want To But They Will — HELD OVER AGAIN — THE RAMONES C.B.G.B. THURS. – SUN. 315 Bowery

of course Greg Shaw's *Who Put the Bomp* magazine, which covered all that good stuff. As you
know, "punk rock" basically meant "garage
rock" to most people back then.'

Visually, the Ramones' image set them apart
from any other band on the mid-Seventies
musical landscape as much as as their buzzsaw
sonic attack. Such singularity was the very
essence of the group. 'We've always been our
own breed of band. We concocted a unique
sound and style all our own trademark,' Joey
later attested. Their adoption of Fifties-style
leather jackets was a rejection of the Seventies'
brushed-denim-and-velvet-jacket executive boogie.

In Johnny's case, the uniform was simply an extension of his everyday attire. 'I had
mine since '67,' he asserts. 'I was a real punk. I was a bad person.' As Legs McNeil
recalls, 'We went to see the Ramones at CBGB's. We were wearing these nerdy t-shirts
and denim jackets. It was embarrassing. The Ramones were wearing leather jackets:
Joey has said they got it from *The Wild One* [the seminal Fifties biker film, starring
Marlon Brando]. I walked out the next day and bought my first. It was a return to the
Fifties . . . The Fonz was on TV – in the first episodes of *Happy Days* he wore a wind-
breaker because it was too threatening for him to wear a leather jacket. Nobody in New
York wore black leather, if you wore one the streets parted in front of you.'

By June 1974 the Ramones had enhanced their line-up to become a quartet,
installing the band's de facto manager, Tommy Erdelyi, as drummer. Prior to being
inducted, Tommy had produced their early demos and distributed flyers promoting the
band's first concerts. This re-arrangement particularly suited Joey – who had a cymbal-
thrashing drum technique described by Tommy as 'eccentric', and was far more interested in fronting the band than supplying rhythm.

'He had such power that he was known to go through the hardware,' Tommy recalls.
'You couldn't hear the rest of the group,' added Johnny. 'I didn't really want to be playing drums,' Joey explained. 'After it didn't work out . . . we tried to find a beat keeper
– a simple kind of drummer. But everybody was kind of flamboyant in those days. So
Tommy would sit behind the drums and show them how to play until we finally asked
him to be the drummer. He said, "OK" and in doing so created the style that drummers
like Paul Cook and everybody else have tried to emulate.'

Likewise, Dee Dee was finding that the high-octane vocal style dictated by the band's
music was shredding his voice – so Joey took over on vocals.

Tommy Ramone was born Tommy Erdelyi on 29 January 1949 in Budapest, Hungary.
His family emigrated to the USA in 1956 and settled in Forest Hills. Tommy attended

Tommy Ramone in Michigan, 1977 – he was happier behind a mixing desk than a drum kit.

Forest Hills High (most notable for providing a fictional education for Peter Parker, aka Spider-Man), where he met Johnny. The duo hit it off immediately, sharing common musical interests, and soon began rehearsing together.

Recalling the period, Tommy explains, 'I met John in the High School cafeteria, somebody introduced me to him. And he charmed me; he's a very charismatic fellow. We were in several bands together in High School, the most famous of which was the Tangerine Puppets. Then, after High School, we kind of drifted apart and went our separate ways. But he would call me up every now and then on the phone to see what was going on, and I would always ask him what he was doing, whether he was playing, and he said he wasn't playing. And I said, "Why don't you play? You should be in a band," because I always thought he had the right kind of personality and charm to be in a rock band. So one day he calls me up and he tells me he'd bought a guitar. I said, "Great, fabulous." He told me he was playing with Dee Dee and I said "Great. This is just what I've been waiting for," because I always thought that these colourful people from Forest Hills would make an exciting unit.'

Of all the Ramones, it was Tommy who had the most accomplished musical background. He was something of a multi-instrumentalist and an experienced recording engineer, who'd worked at Manhattan's Record Plant with funk fusionist Herbie Hancock, the hippie ensemble Mountain, and Jimi Hendrix's post-Experience project, the Band of Gypsys. Tommy also worked at a film company, and this steady employment afforded him the funds to buy a share in a rehearsal space with another old Forest Hills High schoolmate, Monte Melnick. Melnick had played with Tommy in another local glam band, Butch. Like Erdelyi (who adopted the stage name Scott, or Scotty, Thomas), Melnick had made a career in music, recording a couple of albums as bassist for country-rockers 30 Days Out and opening gigs for the Beach Boys and Captain Beefheart. On discovering that Johnny had bought new equipment and formed a band, Tommy and Monte invited them over to rehearse at the Performance Studio. Erdelyi was immediately impressed. 'Right away, they were very different from anything else,' he testifies.

With a stable line-up, the division of labour was established. Dee Dee and Joey were the creative team, with Dee Dee supplying the bulk of the music and around half of the lyrics. Johnny was responsible for the running of the group. He introduced fines for lateness, and instituted a system wherein each of the four founding members would have a vote on group issues. This role suited Johnny's authoritarian personality, but was to rebound on him in later years as the number of original band members decreased and power struggles ensued. Tommy was the only member with any significant studio experience and was the natural choice for handling recording and promotion.

To me it was an Avant-Garde thing. Then we started getting really good and I said, 'This isn't Avant-Garde this is commercial!' And that's when I started playing drums. When I saw the dollar signs . . . [it] changed the whole sound of the group into the way it is. *Tommy Ramone*

The Ramones ethos was established: they were a gang, unified, with each component part serving the greater whole. Dee Dee, the perennial loner, felt at home with this *esprit de corps*: 'I had become a manic depressive. I was hopeless. I could only laugh at someone else's expense and I thrived on negativity. I can see now how it was only natural that I would gravitate toward Tommy, Joey and Johnny Ramone. They were the obvious creeps of the neighbourhood. All their friends had to be creeps. No one would have pegged any of us as candidates for any kind of success in life.'

The Ramones' debut as a quartet took place on Friday 16 August 1974, at the soon-to-be legendary CBGB's, 315 Bowery, New York. Opened beneath a flophouse in December 1973, the venue was originally a hangout for marines and Hell's Angels and was described by *Rolling Stone* as having an 'ambience of piss and disinfectant'.

CBGB's originally lived up to its initials, hosting bands purveying a mixture of Country, Blue Grass and Blues. Owner Hilly Kristal had been convinced to open up the club for rock acts on Sundays by Television manager Terry Ork. Despite an initial paucity of paying customers, the usually parsimonious hippie club owner persevered with what he describes as 'other music for uplifting gormandisers'.

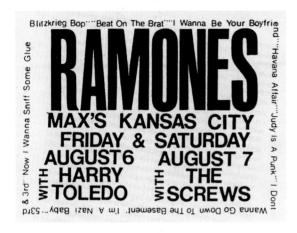

Being local boys, the Ramones soon gravitated towards the bar. 'We were all broke, with nothing,' Joey explained. 'I used to hang out at CBGB's because it was across the street, just to get warm. I'd rather drink a couple of beers, I guess it's nutritious – I couldn't afford to eat so I figured I'd go across the street and have a couple of beers for dinner.'

After Johnny and Tommy hassled Kristal for a gig, the Ramones were booked on the same bill as Angel and the Snakes – a short-lived ensemble that ultimately developed into Blondie. With Tommy having assumed the position of drummer only a fortnight previously, it was hardly surprising the band were some way shy of their potential.

'They were even worse than Television,' recalls Kristal. 'At that first gig at CBGB, they were the most untogether group I'd ever heard. They kept starting and stopping – equipment breaking down – and yelling at each other. They were a mess.'

Regardless, the band rattled through their ten-song set in slightly less than twenty minutes. 'The audience looked like a bunch of glowing Jack o' Lanterns,' observed Dee Dee. 'People were just dying to hear what we did. We had a four-way chemistry that was insane.'

Despite performing for a crowd of less than a hundred – most of whom got in for nothing and were described by Tommy as 'the zoo of the world' – Kristal had faith in the band. As Johnny later recalled, 'He [Kristal] said, "Nobody likes you guys, but I see something there . . . everybody else hates you."

Hilly was to book the band for a further 24 nights before the year was out. Happy to be learning in public, Joey was similarly undaunted by the lack of paying customers. 'There was no one there,' he recalled. 'I think one of our original fans was Alan Vega [of electro-punk pioneers Suicide]. He told Johnny he'd been waiting all his life for this. We'd get a lot of the Warhol types . . . . It was word of mouth in the early days.'

The Ramones' unique but simple sound distilled a wide range of pop-cultural influences, from comic books to B-movies via bubblegum pop and proto-punk. Their lyrics were succinct, repetitious, direct and infectious. In terms of content, they spliced catchy chant-along choruses onto

Max's Kansas City cocktail menu.

a bizarro vision of New York, populated by freaks, geeks, mental patients and pinheads. These songs were performed in staccato bursts of sonic energy that reduced the three-minute pop song to a 60-second motif.

Dressed in near-identical leather jackets, with long dark hair, ripped jeans and white sneakers, the group also combined visual elements of Fifties rockers, Sixties mods and Seventies proto-punks to transform themselves into a collective visual icon. As *NME* journalist Charles Shaar Murray observed in 1975, 'they're representing the Fifties and Sixties in a way that could only be the Seventies.'

The Ramones' pop-cultural *gestalt* was in direct contrast to their 'dumb' image. But the label stuck to the band from its inception. Their limited musical proficiency, uncomplicated song structure and lack of pretension were cited as an absence of creative intelligence. Although the Ramones' minimalism could be viewed as a form of satire, the humour in many of their lyrics led some to dismiss them as a novelty act.

Rebellious rock and roll was punk rock. Gene Vincent, Elvis Presley. That was punk rock. The Beatles in Hamburg, before they put on their suits and were wearing their leather jackets. But by 1974, progressive rock had diluted rock and roll. Everyone had gotten so overindulgent. All of a sudden, we started playing, and other bands saw us play and were inspired. Our main influences would have been the early and mid-Sixties British movement, the Beach Boys, and surf music – pure rock and roll. *Johnny Ramone*

While fellow CBGB's performer Patti Smith hailed the influence of Arthur Rimbaud upon her art, the Ramones offered up the war comics of Joe Kubert or Roger Corman's exploitation films as influences on their 'choons'. This, of course, was part of the game. In actuality, Johnny was an astute, business-orientated motivator; Joey was an intelligent student of popular culture; Tommy was an experienced session man and studio whiz, and Dee Dee the Lord Byron of the group – a creative maverick. As Tommy later told *NME*, 'it wasn't four morons.'

Like most bands, the Ramones were a product of their times. They embraced the elements that appealed to them and disregarded the extraneous. The post-Watergate, post-student activist disillusionment with politics, or societal change of any kind, was reflected in the negativity of songs like 'I Don't Care' and 'Now I Wanna Sniff Some Glue'. If the Ramones could be said to stand for anything at all, it was the feelings of the

Ramones very live at Friars from the Aylesbury Roxette, *June 1977.*

archetypal bored teenager. As Joey explained, 'It's all about passion, real feelings. It's not about, "Yeah, I'm a punk and I'm angry." That's just a lot of crap.'

Joey and Dee Dee had spent much of their youth immersed in TV action series, cartoons and war films, or listening to bubblegum music on transistor radios. These influences naturally seeped through into their songs, as did the do-it-yourself rock 'n' roll ethic that prevailed in the late Fifties and early Sixties. Just as with Eddie Cochran and Gene Vincent, Johnny, Joey and Dee Dee had purchased whatever instrumentation they could afford and started making a noise. The Ramones were about rock 'n' roll, getting loaded, and having fun.

We thought we were a bubblegum band . . . there was no punk movement. *Joey Ramone*

Some commentators insist that they invented punk rock, while others point to more obscure acts. Despite anything former Sex Pistols manager Malcolm McLaren would have us believe, however, the truth is that 'punk', like most genre-specific labels, was only applied retrospectively. The Ramones were the sum total of their musical influences and geographical location. Despite early negative responses, as word of mouth raised their profile so confidence within the group grew. As Johnny recalled, 'We knew what we had. We thought we could be the biggest band in the world.'

In Liverpool, 1977 (Johnny, Tommy, Joey, Dee Dee).

Do Your Parents Know You're Ramones?

Musicians are technical, the Ramones aren't technical.

Monte Melnick

Rock 'n' roll is very primitive, it's not high-tech.

Joey Ramone

As the Ramones' concerts at CBGB's created a growing buzz, they began to gather people who were necessary to take them away from the corner of Bowery and Bleecker Street.

They didn't need to look far for their first employee. Arturo Vega was an artist who occupied a loft on East Second Street, directly around the corner from CBGB's. Described by Joey as 'a creative Mexican', Vega had discovered the band prior to meeting Dee Dee through a neighbour, Sweet Pam, who worked as a dancer for shock-rock transvestite theatre ensemble the Cockettes.

'I love rock 'n' roll but at the time there weren't any exciting things around, so I wandered through the town's clubs looking for something new,' Vega recollects, 'then I saw the Ramones and thought they were good but too funny to be real.' Arturo developed a friendship with the bassist, and Dee Dee, who was usually looking for a place to crash, moved into his apartment.

Joey also washed up at Arturo's loft. He stayed significantly longer than his bandmate, who Vega evicted after becoming tired of the drugs, women and fighting that accompanied Dee Dee wherever he went. 'He put up with a lot of craziness,' admitted Dee Dee later, 'but he was crazy too. Eventually I think he formed a resentment towards me.'

'I didn't like the dope,' Vega explained, 'but I did it a couple of times with Dee Dee. The first time he shot me up, I couldn't move. I couldn't get up. And I felt like throwing up. I was so drowsy and sick and I was talking like you hear junkies talk in the street.'

The Ramones outside CBGB's, 1977 (Dee Dee, Tommy, Johnny, Joey).

New York's finest ride the subway (Dee Dee, Joey, Tommy, Johnny).

Initially hired as a roadie, Arturo graduated to controlling the stage lighting and becoming the Ramones' artistic director. He designed the classic Ramones logo, based upon the presidential seal, and handled all the artwork for flyers and merchandise – the t-shirts he designed were credited with keeping the band afloat during times of hardship. Vega would remain with the band throughout their career, and is still webmaster of the official Ramones site.

Like Vega, Monte Melnick was crucial to the Ramones' development. As manager of the Performance Studio he was involved with the group from their inception, and controlled lighting and sound at the venue when they performed there in November and December 1974. The Studio was also used for rehearsals and recordings by Blondie and former New York Dolls frontman David Johansen.

Despite being initially horrified by the Ramones' lack of musicality, the amiable Melnick found himself helping his business partner, Tommy Erdelyi, by acting as the band's soundman and roadie. He quickly became indispensable as the band's effective den mother, resolving petty hassles, organising schedules and helping Johnny keep the whole show on the road. Melnick was also appointed tour manager, a position he held until the Ramones played their final show in 1997. Like Vega, he continued his involvement after they split, acting as 'co-ordinator', setting up Dee Dee and later Ramones drummer Marky's various live shows – both individually and collectively, as the Remainz.

The Ramones saw out 1974 with a 20 December concert at the Performance Studio, and the recording of their first demo. They laid down most of the tracks that were to appear on their debut album, plus two that never made it: 'It Can't Be', a fairly leaden number featuring a riff that later resurfaced in 'Chinese Rocks', and 'I Don't Wanna Be Learned'/'I Don't Wanna Be Tamed'. (With a running time of almost exactly one minute, 'Learned' is the Ramones at their most reductive, the lyrics consisting of little more than the title while the music features all of the three chords in their repertoire.) The demo was made in less than eight hours with no frills – an approach that became the group's standard practice. The sound was without embellishment, representing the band's live sound at a lesser velocity, the most significant difference from *Ramones* being that Dee Dee's bass is far clearer on the demo.

Tommy and Arturo Vega put together a promotional pack featuring the demo tape, a photograph and some flyer art. The packs were duly mailed out, before the year ended with the band temporarily out of action. (Tommy was run over by a cab, and Johnny spent New Year's Eve in hospital with appendicitis.)

Johnny was keen to build some hype around the Ramones, and had nagged Tommy to target journalists who might be sympathetic. Among these was *Soho Weekly News* columnist Danny Fields. 'We'd seen his name on all these MC5 and Stooges albums,' says Johnny. 'We didn't know who he was or what he did, but we figured that if he liked them, maybe he'd like us.'

We play short songs and short sets for people who don't have a lot of spare time. *Tommy Ramone*

Described by *SWN* colleague Kenneth Tucker as 'the Gertrude Stein of the New York Underground', Fields was also the co-editor of *16 Magazine* and had a wealth of contacts within major record companies. During the late 1960s, Fields had been employed by Elektra Records, where he signed and managed both the MC5 and the Stooges. He was sacked for defending the MC5's First Amendment right to use the word 'fuck' on a record sleeve, then took a similar job with Atlantic Records – only to be fired for criticising the label's prime cash cow, Emerson, Lake and Palmer.

Irrespective of Tommy's promotional blurb, promising 'every song a hit single', there was no stampede to sign the band. A steady trickle of rejections heightened their impression of themselves as outsiders – a gang of 'brudders' against the world. As Fields would later explain, 'The Ramones hated just about every other band in the world, especially ones that were getting written about in early 1975, while they were being ignored.'

After spending the early weeks of the New Year rehearsing, the Ramones returned to the stage on Valentine's Day with a show at Brandy's in Manhattan, followed by another concert at the Performance Studio a fortnight later. In early March they returned to CBGB's for the first of a series of short residencies. *Village Voice* rock critic Robert

Christgau was one of those won over by the foursome's frantic minimalism: 'For me, it was a life changing experience. These four inept sounding geeks had figured out what the Stooges had done wrong – the expressionistic stuff, the long and the slow and the chaos for its own sake. Over the next four years I would see the Ramones more than I've ever seen any band.'

During the ten-week gap between their CBGB shows, appearances by Patti Smith, the Heartbreakers, Suicide, Television, Talking Heads and Blondie suggested a scene was developing around Hilly Kristal's grotty bar. It was at this point that Johnny and Tommy's targeting of Danny Fields began to pay off.

Lisa Robinson, the editor of *Hit Parader* and *Rock Scene* was, like Fields, on the Ramones' hit list. 'I think we had a list of 100 people and hit everybody,' recalls Johnny. 'Lisa Robinson came down and brought more people. She left after the first set and came back for the second set with more people from other magazines.'

Both Robinson and Fields had been receiving mail-outs from another band playing on the same night, so they agreed that she should go see the Ramones. Robinson found their approach revelatory: 'I really loved Led Zeppelin, but after spending several tours with them and watching lengthy guitar and drum solos, I saw the Ramones, with all

Johnny and Joey assume the position.

their songs under three minutes, and thought it was such a refreshing change. I thought that they were really charming, and that, for the time, their energy was a much needed shot in the arm.'

The next day Robinson phoned Fields to insist that he too see the Ramones. 'She knew my attention span wasn't very long,' he recalls. 'I guess she liked the idea that they had a gimmick – a great name, they all wore jeans and white t-shirts and black leather jackets, and sneered. It sounded very good to me, so I went to see them.'

Fields' reaction was overwhelmingly enthusiastic. 'They're a very professional group, they work very hard, and I thought, "It's like the Stooges without the curse of Iggy."' Immediately after the show he met the band and offered to become their manager.

This was a huge step forward for the Ramones. They were making very little money from playing live (a gig with Johnny Thunders' Heartbreakers had seen the two bands split the $50 take), and the demo was reported to have cost them nearly a thousand dollars. Joey was still on welfare, Johnny was carrying his Mosrite around in a plastic shopping bag, and the band's initial choice, former New York Dolls manager Marty Thau, had turned them down in favour of working as a producer.

The Bowery was a drab, ugly and unsavoury place. But it was good enough for rock 'n' rollers. The people who frequented CBGB's didn't seem to mind staggering drunks and stepping over a few bodies. *Hilly Kristal —*

Characteristically, Johnny elicited a promise of new equipment before any deal was struck. The Ramones were shortly better off to the tune of one new drum kit and an experienced manager.

Top of Fields' agenda was getting the band a record deal. To this end, an audition was arranged with the independent Sire label on 23 June, followed by Blue Sky (Fields had worked for label owner Steve Paul's management company) and Arista, who had recently signed Patti Smith. Logically enough, given the infectiousness of their songs, Sire wanted to offer the band a singles deal – with 'You're Gonna Kill That Girl' as the first release. However, both Fields and the Ramones wanted an album deal.

'Many of the so called "knowledgeable" A&R men of the day enjoyed attending Ramones shows but weren't certain they were recordable,' observed Marty Thau. 'None of the New York punk scene acts had been signed to a label, and everyone was watching and waiting to see if the new movement had legs. One major A&R chieftain said, "If this punk garbage ever hits, I will leave the business." The music business really missed the boat on the Ramones – people who should have known better ended up looking rather pathetic.'

Steve Paul was keen to take a chance on them, but wanted to see the Ramones perform in a larger setting than the intimate surroundings of CBGB's or the Performance Studio. He hastily arranged for the band to be added to the bill of a Johnny Winter show, on 11 July at the Palace Theatre in Waterbury, Connecticut. It was to be the Ramones' first major support engagement, as well as their debut show outside of New York. It was also something of a nightmare.

Johnny Winter's crowd were mainly ageing rockers who were right up for some fairly traditional, well executed, blues-tinged axe worship. When support band the Stories finished their set, the stage lights went up for what was expected to be the main event. However, the Ramones had been added to the bill at the last minute, with no mention of them on posters or tickets. When the 2,000-strong crowd realised this was most definitely *not* Johnny Winter, they stopped cheering and laid siege to the band. 'I've never got so many bottles, or firecrackers, or people giving me the finger,' recalled Dee Dee. 'The people were just so upset with us, and after that we didn't want to play anymore. We said, "Forget it, this is no fun." But we were too involved to turn back.'

Despite his initial horrified reaction, Hilly Kristal had by now warmed to the Ramones. Equally excited by some of the other acts he was putting on, he resolved to hold a festival of this new music.

'I went through my list of some 250 bands and advertised for auditions. I picked the most original and best of these bands and entitled it "A Festival of the Top 40 New York Rock Bands,"' Kristal explained. 'People were amazed at how many good new bands there were and came back many times. They started to hang out, getting into this new rock music.'

Putting together a bill that also included Television, the Heartbreakers, Blondie and Talking Heads, Kristal took out large ads in *The Village Voice* and *Soho Weekly News*. The three nights of sold-out gigs also attracted attention from the UK, courtesy of Lisa Robinson working as the *NME*'s stateside editor. The 7 June edition of the British music weekly had already featured a prominent article on the New York scene by Robinson. Centred on the drag-rock theatrics of Wayne County, the article presented pen-portraits of the scene's main players, including the Ramones. Whereas County dismissed them as 'old fashioned', Robinson described them as '*The* most amazing new band I've heard yet.' It acted as a primer for a British audience that was questioning the relevance of an ageing rock hierarchy, looking for a new kick.

Taking place over one weekend in July 1975, the CBGB's festival has been mythologised as the birthing chamber of punk rock – in much the same way that the 100 Club festival (featuring the Sex Pistols, the Damned and Siouxsie and the Banshees) is viewed as the British scene's defining moment.

Heavily attended by A&R men and journalists, the festival gave the CBGB's scene a form and identity in the press. The Ramones' ferocity was captured by *Village Voice* reviewer James Wolcott, who observed; 'Like the Wild Bunch, the Ramones leave nothing behind them but scorched earth. Typical set begins with Joey curled around the mike-stand announcing, "I Don't Want To Go Down To The Basement", a romp quickly followed by "California Sun" and "Beat On The Brat", the set ending ferociously with "I Wanna Be Your Boyfriend", all songs played with a chopping freneti-

A sensitive shot of Joey from 1977.

cism, the pace is so brutal that the audience can barely catch its breath, much less applaud. A Ramones rampage is intoxicating – it's exciting to hear the voltage sizzle – but how long can they keep it up? Maybe that's why their sets average twenty minutes.'

The Ramones had not announced themselves to the world as 'punks'. Indeed, at the time of the CBGB's festival, the term was yet to be applied to anything other than 1960s garage rock. The sounds that cut the stale air of Hilly's club were initially pigeonholed as 'street rock' – apt enough in the case of the Ramones, the Heartbreakers, or even Blondie, though Talking Heads and Television owed more to the boulevard than the street. It was the stripped down, no-frills aesthetic that would become influential to punk, by virtue of timing and location.

The first coupla times I saw the group play, I must say I didn't like 'em, but I got used to it although it took some time. But then, I guess the first time some people taste champagne they wanna spit it out, right? Still, I think they oughta put more different things in their music, 'n' complicate it up a bit, if they wanna get high up on the whaddayacallit – the lists, the charts? *Noel Hyman*

The Fifties and Sixties fashion elements employed by the Ramones, the Heartbreakers and Blondie gave each band an identifiable image. Leather jackets, ripped t-shirts, straight ties and black jeans manifested a look that was identifiable both in the bands and in the audience. As the *New York Times'* John Rockwell reported, 'This is yet another group in what has become a fixed New York pattern. Black leather jackets, a parodistic macho camp swagger, and furious blasting rock and roll. But what the Ramones offer is non-stop energy (based on double-time guitar strumming), a few clever hooks, and sudden start-and-stop endings to their songs. For all the underground image, this is a band with obvious commercial potential, and one imagines that potential will start being realised very soon.'

For the Ramones, however, becoming the exemplars of a nascent musical revolution must have seemed very distant. In the high summer of 1975, Johnny still wanted a record deal and Dee Dee needed to score.

Although he'd declined to manage the Ramones, Marty Thau made it clear he'd welcome the opportunity to record the band. A two-track demo featuring 'Judy Is A Punk' and 'I Wanna Be Your Boyfriend' was recorded at the 914 Studio in New York on 19 September. Thau produced the tracks in a straightforward live style, with Johnny's guitar lower down in the mix than on *Ramones*. (Oddly though, the producer chose to end 'Judy Is A Punk' with a flourish of swirling piano.)

Johnny – the Leader of the Pack, 1976.

Describing the band's music as 'high energy minimalism', Thau passed a copy of the tape to Sire producer/A&R man Craig Leon, who played it to company head Seymour Stein. Leon was familiar with most of the bands on the scene. 'I initially went to CBGB's because I was trying to sign Patti Smith,' he later explained. 'She went with Arista because they were a much bigger label, but while chasing her I noticed that there were all these other bands playing at CBGB's so I started going there regularly to check them out. I found a number of really interesting bands who, like Patti, were in their own ways trying to recapture the spirit of rock and roll, which was kind of dead at that time, and infuse their rock and roll with some of the ideas of the Fifties and the earlier art and poetry scenes of NY and Europe.'

Leon felt that the Ramones were 'exactly the opposite of all the pretentious music that was coming out at the time', and his enthusiasm was shared by Stein. Despite the band's rejection of his singles deal, Stein had liked what he'd seen at the audition and remained interested. He'd founded Sire with writer and producer Richard Gotteherer in 1966. The label had been financially underpinned in the 1970s by profits from the US publishing rights to Fleetwood Mac's back catalogue, and the output of Dutch prog-rockers Focus. Beset by distribution problems and keen to establish a roster of dynamic young acts, Stein had been monitoring the Ramones' progress through Leon.

'There were two bands that I really thought were gonna happen out of New York at that time,' Leon explains, 'and they were the Ramones and Talking Heads. I saw both of them on the same night and brought them in to Sire and I was producing the Ramones album in '75 and '76.'

An arrangement had been made for Stein to see the band perform at Mother's, a New York gay bar, where the Ramones and Blondie were playing three nights at the start of October. Stein came down with flu and was too sick to attend, but his ex-wife, Linda Stein, took his place, and her enthusiasm for the band kicked Sire's interest into high gear.

As Joey explains, 'Stein was willing to take chances when nobody else was. After us he signed Talking Heads, the Dead Boys and Richard Hell.' However, the Ramones' lyrical use of Nazi imagery did give Stein pause for thought. After some discussion with the band, and with Fields (with whom Stein had enjoyed a long professional association), he decided, 'Sire wasn't the kind of record company, and I wasn't the sort of music person, to restrict anything, and I went along with it.'

The way in which the band referred to fascism was all to do with shock tactics and their collective sense of humour, rather than ideological dogma. Lyrics such as 'I'm a shock trooper in a stupor' and 'I'm a Nazi schatze, y'know I fight for the Fatherland' (from 'Today Your Love, Tomorrow The World') were simply too absurd to be taken seriously by anyone not suffering from a critically diminished sense of irony. 'It just sounded good, it wasn't political,' insisted Johnny. He may have had an authoritarian manner and conservative leanings, but it would be a quantum leap to call Johnny a fascist.

'I thought the Ramones lyrics were funny,' Danny Fields admitted. 'I mean Dee Dee wasn't talking about the extermination of a race, it was more a one-on-one thing, you know, "when the bedroom door closes, I'm a Nazi." Dee Dee grew up in Germany, Dee

The preying mantis of punk – Joey in 1976.

Dee was intrigued. He was like a kid saying a dirty word to see if he got his mouth washed out with soap.'

Indeed, Dee Dee first linked his childhood fascination with fascist regalia with rock-'n' roll when he saw the swastika on the back of Stooges drummer Scott Asheton's jacket. Lighting/artistic director Arturo Vega also produced day-glo images of swastikas in a distinctly ambiguous context. 'The more I got into my swastika paintings, the more I really thought about them,' Vega explained. 'The paintings are a closet Nazi detector, you know? They bring out the Nazi in you if you're a closet Nazi, because the people that are gonna be offended are the ones that have something to hide. The people that act so defensively are always the ones that are closet fascists. That's why the paintings are so beautiful – they find you out.'

As *Punk* magazine writer (and later film director) Mary Harron recalled, 'I would have arguments about this stuff. Arturo had some really nasty ideas, but Joey Ramone was a nice guy, he was no savage right-winger. The Ramones were problematic. It was hard to work out what their politics were. It had this difficult edge, but the most important thing was needling the older generation. Hating hippies was the big thing.'

The Ramones eventually signed a five-year deal with Sire records in January 1976. As the band were now contracted to produce an album a year, their debut album was scheduled to begin recording the following month. Tommy paid tribute to Craig Leon in getting the band a recording contract: 'He brought down the vice president and all these people – he's the only hip one at the record company. He risked his career to get us on the label.' But Sire signed the Ramones for an advance of only $6,000, with additional funds for expenses and equipment. The deal was effectively financed by Stein's sale of the sub-publishing rights to Chapel Music, indicative of the label's financial problems. In an era when dinosaur supergroups spent hundreds of thousands of dollars recording their self-indulgent 'masterworks', the Ramones had been picked up for peanuts.

Johnny's high-octane guitar technique in motion – on stage with Joey, 1977.

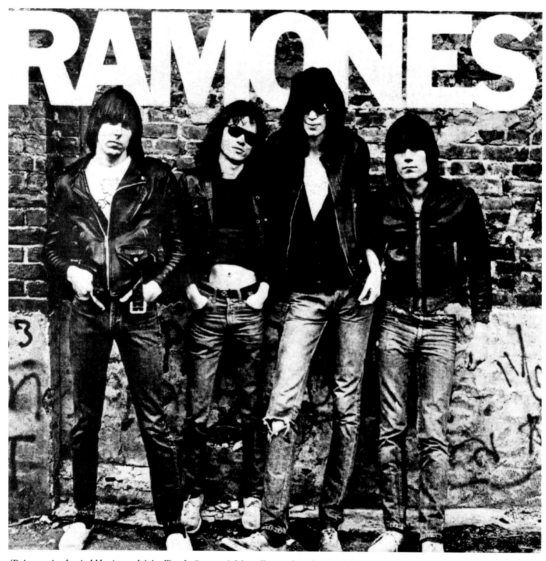

'Driven, primal, mind blasting rock 'n' roll' – the Ramones' debut album, released in April 1976.

Three Chords, Four Leather Jackets

All I wanted to do was make one album and go back to my job as a construction worker. *Johnny Ramone*

In keeping with the band's penchant for brevity, the Ramones' debut album was recorded and mixed in less than seven weeks.

Sessions began on 2 February 1976 at Plaza Sound, a cavernous (65' x 100' x 30') 1930s-style rehearsal space that came complete with a pipe organ. The studio was situated within Radio City Music Hall, and had been used to rehearse big bands and dancers during the golden age of radio.

Production was handled by Craig Leon, with assistance from Tommy. While the band had more than enough songs for an album, their simple structures and the similarity to live Ramones performances ensured it was completed by 19 February, at a cost of less than $6,500.

The band had been booked into the cheaper evening sessions and spent less than three days in the studio – with half of the album being laid down on day one. This delighted Johnny, who stuck to the precedent of spending no more time in the studio than was absolutely necessary. 'We laid out the basic tracks in two days,' he testified, 'no overdubs on the vocals. We went through four or five songs in one take. No bullshit, no politics, just rock 'n' roll.' As Seymour Stein later observed, 'If everyone was like them, record companies would have no worries.'

The recording and editing process was equally direct. 'A lot of "experts" said the band couldn't be recorded,' explains Leon. 'In fact the band was quite chaotic live but we got around that with quite a few rehearsal sessions (mainly to figure out how to end the songs which used to be played in one long blur in their live set) . . . the recording techniques that we used in the studio were extremely conservative, using the same classical mic techniques and approach that George Martin applied to early Beatles recordings.'

Describing Leon's approach, Joey explained, 'Guitar and drums in one channel, bass and vocals in another, gave it a ping-pong effect.' Leon added very little in the way of additional instrumentation, but the studio's pipe organ was used to good effect on the cover of Chris Montez's 1962 hit 'Let's Dance'. Some tubular bells, extra guitar and

glockenspiel were incorporated into the sentimental 'I Wanna Be Your Boyfriend', and the eponymous power tool was dubbed onto the run-in of 'Chainsaw'.

Leon's overdubbing of Johnny's guitar gave the songs a textured, whooshing effect. 'I wanted to hear the impact of a Ronettes record without having 300 things playing,' he explains. The guitar sound achieved on *Ramones* is markedly different to that found on any of the band's later albums, inspired by the technique used by Hawkwind guitarist Dave Brock on the acid-metal band's early recordings.

Leon also experimented with microphone placement to make Tommy's drum sound fuller: 'We just took a pair of grand pianos and put them around Tommy's kit and put bricks on their sustain pedals. Then we

THE RAMONES ARE SO PUNKY
YOU'RE GONNA HAVE TO REACT!

THEIR MUSIC'S SWEPT THE BOWERY...
NOW IT'S GONNA SWEEP THE COUNTRY!

Advertisement for Ramones *from* New York Rocker.

put up a pair of 87's [Neumann U microphones] in a normal pattern over the drums, cranked them up, limited them to death, had him do one hit, and it sounds like cannons exploding.'

Ramones featured many of the tracks that were to become fan favourites and a stable of 'da brudders'' repetoire for the next two decades. As with their live set, 'Blitzkrieg Bop' was the opener – a foot-stomping slice of bubblegum punk. The song was written by Tommy, title courtesy of Dee Dee. 'It's an ode to the rock 'n' roll fan,' explained the drummer/co-producer. 'It's about having a good time at a music show, the excitement of seeing your favourite band. It's about fans and bands, a love letter to the fans.' Tommy's lyrics also contained the couplet that became one of the Ramones' catchphrases. '"Hey ho, let's go" was the battle cry that sounded the revolution, a call to arms for punks to do their own thing,' enthused Joey.

'Beat On The Brat' extolled the virtues of beating on brats with baseball bats, and introduced the world to the Ramones' trademark dumb humour. Explaining the observational nature of his lyric, Joey recalled, 'I was living in Forest Hills, walking around the neighbourhood, annoyed by all these rich ladies with their bratty kids.' As a promotional gimmick, Sire later produced miniature bats bearing the song title.

The Ramones survey the Bowery, 1977.

On the album's third track, 'Judy Is A Punk', the Ramones cemented their association with the burgeoning subculture that had only recently been labelled 'punk'. The song was the first in a mini-genre that would include 'Suzy Is A Headbanger' and 'Sheena Is A Punk Rocker', before the concept was exhausted with 'Heidi Is A Head Case' on their final studio album, *Adios Amigos*. With a running time of slightly less than 29 minutes, *Ramones* was a whistle-stop introduction to bubblegum punk.

The writing credits on *Ramones* established a policy of collective anonymity, with all songs simply attributed to 'the Ramones'. 'Everything was credited to the band to create a sense of unity,' explained Joey, 'and we will always be a unit, a bonded kind of band.'

Irrespective of such bonds, individual songs were later attributed to individual members. '53rd & 3rd' is based on Dee Dee's experience of hustling for tricks on the intersection of those two streets. '"53rd & 3rd" is a chilling song,' observed Legs Mc Neil. 'It's about this guy standing on the corner of 53rd and Third, trying to hustle guys, but nobody ever picks him. Then when somebody does, he kills the john to prove that he's not a sissy.' Entirely written by the bassist, it's indicative of Dee Dee's more visceral approach. As he explained, 'The song speaks for itself, everything I write is autobiographical and very real. I can't write any other way.'

What's brevity mean? _Johnny Ramone_

'Now I Wanna Sniff Some Glue', 'I Don't Wanna Go Down To The Basement' and 'Loudmouth' explore what would become familiar topics of Dee Dee's songs: substance abuse, boredom, horror films, violence, and problems with women.

On the other hand, Joey's lyrics leant towards humour ('Beat On The Brat') and bubblegum romance ('Listen To My Heart'). Inspired by the cult horror film *The Texas Chainsaw Massacre*, 'Chainsaw' describes Joey's woe at the loss of his 'baby' to Leatherface and his family. Had Dee Dee written the lyric, the song would undoubtedly have taken on a more violently literal context. As it was, Johnny's guitar (which segues seamlessly out of the overdubbed power saw at the start of the track) provided a cutting-edge counterpoint to Joey's understated vocal. When the Ramones made their Los Angeles debut at the Roxy in August 1976, Joey introduced 'Chainsaw' as 'a love song'.

In addition to 'Blitzkrieg Bop', Tommy contributed 'I Wanna Be Your Boyfriend' – the closest thing on *Ramones* to a ballad. As he later told journalist David Fricke, 'I wrote "I Wanna Be Your Boyfriend" because we had all these other songs with "I Don't Wanna" – "I Don't Wanna Walk Around With You", "I Don't Wanna Go Down To The Basement". The only other positive song we had was "Now I Wanna Sniff Some Glue". One thing we all had in common was we were frustrated. We escaped from our anger with humour. A lot of that came from Dee Dee's sensibility, this Dada sensibility that got squeezed down into "I Don't Wanna."'

'I Wanna Be Your Boyfriend' allowed the sensitivity and emotion in Joey's voice to be heard for the first time, juxtaposed with the chiming fuzz of Johnny's guitar. (Backing

'Beat on the Brat' – Dee Dee takes it on the chin, 1977.

vocals were provided by producer Leon and engineer Rob Freeman, who'd later collaborate on Blondie's early albums for Sire, *Blondie* and *Plastic Letters*.)

Ramones was sent to Sterling Sound to produce acetate master copies, where it was discovered that the album had been recorded at such intense volume that the cutter head bored straight through the acetate disc – ripping itself to pieces in the process. Although this was partly attributed to the inexperience of engineer Greg Calbi (who was blamed for setting the recording levels too high, thus causing the needle carrying the sound to push through the disc), Sire made good copy out of the incident in the album's press release.

Johnny, Tommy and Joey in Holland, 1977.

All that *Ramones* now needed was a cover. Initial attempts at photographing the band had not gone well, and the entire budget of $2,000 had been eaten up by images that nobody liked. The Ramones were reluctant photographic subjects, unsettled by the artifice of posing and wanting to get it over with in the shortest possible time.

'We were never comfortable,' Johnny later observed, 'and I still feel very foolish doing it. You want the band to look cool, because image is very important, and the photographer says, "Do something!" But we don't do nothing. You don't want to put your arms around somebody, so you all just stand there.'

Fortunately, the band were less reluctant to be photographed by Roberta Bayley for the newly launched *Punk* magazine. Scheduled to appear in the April edition (number three), Bayley's shots came to the attention of Sire who bought all three rolls of images for $125. The print they selected was to become an iconic representation of the band.

Within eighteen months it would become a cliché for punk bands to be pictured, in grainy black and white, looking surly/moody/bored against a liberally graffitied urban background. Variations on the theme would include the Heartbreakers' seminal *L.A.M.F.* album, which depicts the band framed by two brick walls on either side of an alley, and the Dead Boys' debut, *Young, Loud and Snotty*, which sets them against perpendicular brick walls.

The Ramones weren't the first group to be pictured in such a manner – but the cover photo distilled their accessibility and directness, their image, their lyrical preoccupations and their attitude. Had they not gone on to establish their style with several albums that looked and sounded broadly the same, then the impact of the first cover may never have made *Rolling Stone*'s all-time-100 album sleeves list. The cover of *Ramones* – like the clarion call of 'Hey ho, let's go' – delineates the turning of the mid-1970s musical tide.

Of all the group, Tommy was particularly aware that the Ramones were producing something fresh and unique: 'If we had waited around for the big money, the scene might never have happened, OK? . . . going with a label that can deal with you without having to worry about twenty million other groups on their label is very important when you're starting something new. That's why all the good stuff came out on Elektra in the Sixties . . . all the good stuff in the Fifties came out on Sun and these small independent labels.'

As Joey was later to attest, 'I feel we revolutionised rock and roll. It was something that just happened. I guess in the same way the Beatles didn't know what was going to happen, or Elvis Presley didn't know what was going to happen.'

Ramones was released on 23 April 1976, with a modest launch party – but with no real sense of being part of any new, so-called 'punk' movement. The media had other ideas. While it would be a year before most record stores would incorporate a 'punk rock' section, the bandwagon was ready to roll. *Punk* magazine had hit the stands in January, and would play an important role in defining the genre.

The first album was a statement of rawness – minimal, striking, and unique. *Tommy Ramone*

The magazine was the idea of a young artist, John Holmstrom, who had been inspired by the music of the Dictators in particular and the CBGB's scene in general. Holmstrom was a talented illustrator, who had worked as an apprentice to the great comic book artist Will Eisner (creator of *The Spirit*). After Eisner's studio closed, Holmstrom hooked up with co-founder Ged Dunn Jr., then running a decorating business in their hometown of Cheshire, Connecticut. The youngest of the *Punk* triumvirate, Legs McNeil, was an aspiring filmmaker who hung out with Holmstrom and Dunn after work.

'I hated most rock 'n' roll, because it was about lame hippie stuff,' recalled McNeil, 'and there really wasn't anyone describing our lives – which was McDonalds, beer, and TV reruns. Then John found the Dictators and we all got excited that something was happening.'

Punk magazine's opposition to the hippie scene was indicative of the way in which the Sixties underground had been assimilated. As *Punk* journalist Marry Harron explained, 'Hippie culture had gone very mainstream; for the first time Bohemia embraced fast food. It was about saying "yes" to the modern world. *Punk*, like Warhol, embraced everything that cultured people, and hippies, detested; plastic, junk food, B-movies, advertising, making money – although no one ever did.'

Like Holmstrom, Legs McNeil had been thoroughly rocked by the Dictators' first album, *Go Girl Crazy*, and saw the magazine as a literary embodiment of their d-u-m-b lyricism. He was also responsible for the magazine's soon-to-be-ubiquitous title. 'I said, why don't we call it *Punk*? The word punk seemed to sum up the threat that connected everything we liked – drunk, obnoxious, smart but not pretentious, absurd, funny, ironic, and things that appealed to the darker side.'

'It was all decided in about two seconds,' recalled Holmstrom. 'If you watched cop shows like *Kojak* and *Beretta*, when the cops finally catch the mass-murderer, they'd say, "you dirty punk." It was what your teachers would call you. It meant that you were the lowest. All of us drop-outs and fuck-ups got together and started a movement.'

The etymology of 'punk' extended to the sexual connotations of the word. As

> # John Holmstrom and his living cartoon character, Legs McNeil, were two maniacs running around town putting up signs that said, 'Punk is coming! Punk is coming!' We thought, here comes another shitty group, with an even shittier name. *Deborah Harry*

William Burroughs asserted, in prison parlance, 'a punk was somebody who took it up the ass.' This leant the term a degree of sexual ambiguity, echoed in the lyrics to '53rd & 3rd', as well as the Ramones' adoption of the shrunken t-shirts and ripped jeans often worn by New York's street hustlers.

'I don't think Dee Dee was a full time hustler,' observed Danny Fields. 'I know he wanted girls more than he wanted boys. I thought that was very modern.' MC5 guitarist Wayne Kramer was in jail at the time, and had learnt to be circumspect about his association with punk rock: '. . . one of my pals bought me a subscription to *Billboard* magazine. I started reading about the Ramones, who to me all looked like Fred "Sonic" Smith – and they were managed by Danny Fields. So all these articles kept saying that these kind of bands were inspired by the MC5, and from where I sat, "punk" did not have a good ring to it . . . in jail, a punk is somebody that they knock down and make their girlfriend.'

By November 1975, it was logical that CBGB's would become *Punk* magazine's first port of call. As fortune had it, the Ramones were playing the third night of a weekend residency. 'We had no idea if the Ramones would talk to us that night,' Holmstrom recalls. 'Not only did they agree to talk with us, but we had front row centre seats! It was the Sunday after Thanksgiving and they had played Friday and Saturday as well so there were only around 30-50 people there that night.'

The first issue of *Punk* was published on New Year's Eve 1975, containing interviews

with the Ramones and Lou Reed, a feature on Marlon Brando and Legs McNeil's fictional interview with the cartoon character 'Sluggo'.

Given Holmstrom's artistic background and influences, it's unsurprising that the magazine had a high content of cartoons and *fumetti*, or captioned photo-stories. Much of the photography for the *fumetti* strips and interviews was supplied by Roberta Bayley, who McNeil met on a subsequent visit to CBGB's. Bayley had been going out with Television bassist Richard Hell. When she went along to the venue with the band, manager Terry Ork asked her if she could collect the door money. It led to Hilly Kristal taking her on as permanent door person, affording her unlimited access to the club and its developing scene.

Irrespective of Sire acquiring her Ramones shoot, half a dozen of the pictures found their way into *Punk*, as

An early issue of Punk, *with John Holmstrom's classic cartoon depiction of Joey.*

scheduled. The accompanying interview covered the band's origins and influences, and the cover sported a classic Holmstrom cartoon of Joey. In fact, Holmstrom's memorable cartoons would eventually find their way onto the Ramones' album sleeves – the inner sleeve illustrations to *Rocket To Russia*, and the cover of *Road To Ruin*.

The Bayley image selected for the album cover was one of the least animated of the photo shoot, with Joey slouched against the wall in such a manner that the height difference between himself and the rest of the band was less obvious. The diminutive Tommy is practically *en point*, giving Dee Dee the appearance of an impish younger brudder of comparable height. The back cover was a reproduction of Arturo Vega's ubiquitous American Eagle belt buckle, with the track listing above. The simplicity of the image is matched by the manner in which it was produced: 'I took this photograph with an automatic photo machine,' recalls Vega. 'It cost 25 cents. The kind of machine which you just put a coin in and it takes a picture of you.'

The world at large proved oblivious to both the album and its packaging, however. Initial sales were less than 7,000, and the album peaked at number 111 on the *Billboard* US chart. Reviews were largely favourable, but radio airplay was practically non-existent, particularly outside of New York and California.

In Britain, the ever-prescient John Peel picked up on the album as soon as it was

Diddley, comic books and horror flicks, awkward sex and romantic longing and, in every phrase, the defining moment of saying exactly what you want.'

As *Trouser Press* were later to observe, 'Like all cultural watersheds, *Ramones* was embraced by a discerning few and slagged off as a bad joke by the uncomprehending majority. It is now inarguably a classic.' Regardless of radio hostility and public incomprehension, Joey was simply pleased to have a record on the racks, admitting, 'I've only heard it once. I don't even have a copy. I can't believe it, you know . . . if I turn on the radio and ever hear it, I think I'll go berserk.'

In the 14 June 1976 edition of *The Village Voice*, Robert Christgau described *Ramones* as 'clean the way the [New York] Dolls never were, sprightly the way the Velvets never were, and just plain listenable the way Black Sabbath never was.'

They're simultaneously so funny, such a cartoon vision of rock 'n' roll, and so genuinely tight and powerful, that they will enchant anybody who fell in love with rock 'n' roll for the right reasons. *Charles Shaar Murray,* NME

Over in England, the band were receiving press coverage on a relatively larger scale. *NME*'s Charles Shaar Murray and Kris Needs, in *Zigzag* magazine, amplified the sense of excitement surrounding the Queens quartet. In the 15 May issue of *NME*, Nick Kent gave a resonant description of the album: 'The band itself is hard, tight and extremely limited . . . Drums and bass muscle in behind the guitar, forming a fermenting backdrop for the singer to intone lyrics – every last syllable of which relate to the band's corporate cartoon cut-out overview of Noo Yawk Scuzz, dumb chicks, romance and boredom – in a voice possessing an angloid hyper-thyroid proximity to Rob Tyner's classic mid-register vocals for MC5 records.'

Stateside, Kenneth Tucker in the *Soho Weekly News* was struck by the album's vigour: 'the great joy of their record is the deft transition from one passionate mood to another while maintaining the intensity. I played it constantly when I first got it, and still slap it on for an instant energy rush.'

In *Creem*, Gene Sculatti frothed, '*Ramones* reads like a rock 'n' roll reactionary's manifesto. The kind of driven, primal, mind blasting rock 'n' roll that fuelled Stooges fan clubs . . . The infusion of the Kinks, Herman's Hermits, fake Mersey accents, MC5 and Bay City Rollers into the Ramones' music is all the more crucial, vital to the survival of rock 'n' roll . . .'

But the critical buzz was slow in translating into record sales. 'It almost felt like it never came out,' observed a gloomy Dee Dee, 'it was so anticlimactic to all the fuss about the band.'

In his review, *Circus* magazine's Paul Nelson offered up cautious enthusiasm: 'the

'Gabba, Gabba, we accept you . . . ', Johnny and Joey perform 'Pinhead', 1977.

Ramones represent a kind of idealised Top 40 music . . . an intellectual concept. And one probably having no basis in reality . . . And maybe the kids of America don't want it to. *Ramones* is another chance to find out. I hope the verdict is yes. I hope that whatever doubts I have turn out to be bullshit.'

Unfortunately, Nelson's fears were well-founded. But the level of interest emanating from Britain was enough to convince Sire and Danny Fields that the band may have a ready-made audience waiting for them across the pond.

The Eagle Has Landed

It's a good thing we split from these assholes 200 years ago. I hope they really don't think we sniff glue. I quit when I was eight. *Dee Dee Ramone*

On 4 July 1976, while the rest of America was celebrating the bi-centennial anniversary of the Declaration of Independence, the Ramones headed back to the land of their fore-fathers. They were about to kick off a very different kind of revolution. As Danny Fields later observed, 'Here it was, the 200th anniversary of our freedom from Great Britain, and we were bringing Great Britain this gift that was going to forever disrupt their sensibilities.'

Fields had begun the year struggling to find the band a gig anywhere outside of New York. The swell of negative publicity engulfing anything with the 'punk' tag made it near impossible for the band to sign with an established booking agent. Plans to play in Boston had floundered until Fields came across a rundown bar in the Cambridge district. The owner of Frolics agreed to book the band for a part share in the two-dollar door charge.

Although conditions were less than perfect (the hotel where the band stayed was of the 'no star' variety, and Dee Dee was going through withdrawal), the gig drew a crowd including future collaborator Andy Paley and bubblegum punk Jonathan Richman. Further sorties to Brockton MA, Long Island and New Jersey introduced the band to audiences outside their immediate neighbourhood, interspersed with appearances on home turf at CBGB's and Max's Kansas City.

The deal with Sire had furnished the Ramones with new equipment, including Marshall amps that let them perform at suitably ear-splitting volume. With their debut album in the stores they opened a string of East Coast promotional dates, with two nights supporting English pub rockers Dr Feelgood at the Bottom Line club.

As a showcase for upcoming bands, the Bottom Line was barely larger than CBGB's, and the newly amped Ramones generated enough noise at their soundcheck to bring traffic to a halt outside. But, as *Trouser Press* writer Ira Robins recalls, 'It was their big up-from-the-underground-into-the-mainstream-light gig, and Johnny still had to tune

Touchdown on the big stage. The Ramones with their American Eagle Logo, 1978.

Dee Dee's bass for him, onstage, after they came out.'

It was by now apparent that the level of coverage the Ramones were receiving was far more comprehensive in the UK than at home. The Sex Pistols were at the centre of an embryonic punk scene that had been developing in London over the past twelve months. However, no British punk act had yet made it onto vinyl, and the Clash and the Damned were yet to make their first public appearances.

The British music press had given disproportionate coverage to the handful of low-key gigs played by the Pistols, who started getting copy less than three months after forming. Some saw punk as the Next Big Thing, with hyperbole whipped up by astute managers Malcolm McLaren and Bernard Rhodes, and articles dissecting the roots of this new phenomenon.

The term 'punk rock' had crossed the Atlantic at an early stage, and, by association, the Ramones were identified as trailblazers of the scene. In London during the sweltering summer of 1976 – with the exception of Blondie's debut single, 'X Offender', and a live CBGB's compilation featuring Blondie, Talking Heads, art-rockers Pere Ubu and others – *Ramones* was the only punk record it was possible to buy.

It's great seeing the kids wearing leather jackets and stuff. We're trend-setters. *Dee Dee Ramone*

The album shot to the top of the UK import charts. It was enough to convince both Sire and Danny Fields of the viability of dates in Europe. 'Linda Stein, Seymour Stein's wife, who was my partner in managing the Ramones, was very internationally minded,' recalls Fields. 'She was, I would say, hypnotised – and rightly so, by the lucrative possibilities open to the Ramones on the European market. From the very beginning, she properly sensed that we were likely to find an easier niche in the UK. So from the beginning, we tried to get to England, especially as it seemed less and less likely that we could move beyond New Jersey.'

Charles Shaar Murray had first written about the Ramones for the *NME* in November 1975. Lured to the Performance Studio by coverage in the New York press, he was surprised to find them playing to such small audiences. His enthusiastic report stressed how their 'ridiculously compressed bursts of power chords and hooklines' would produce 'nuthin' but hit singles if there was any justice in this crummy world,' and a desire to see the band 'explode over an unprepared audience at Dingwalls.' He was to be granted his wish on their first trip abroad.

To coincide with Independence Day, a concert at the Roundhouse in north London's Chalk Farm was headlined by the Flamin' Groovies. The Groovies shared the Ramones' enthusiasm for back-to-basics rock, and had been touring Europe since 1972. More conventionally accomplished, however, they viewed the Forest Hill Four as interlopers. The liner notes from the 1993 release *Groovin' At The Roundhouse* described the mood of the occasion:

'While the Groovies were preparing to blitz the world with a high powered dose of rock & roll in the Fifties and Sixties tradition, punk rock had come along in the meantime and largely usurped their mission. *Shake Some Action*, originally recorded in 1972, was released on Sire simultaneously with the first Ramones album in 1976. This led to an unusual kind of tension when the two bands toured England together in the summer of that year. In deference to their seniority, the Groovies headlined over the Ramones and various upstart English bands and the shows were packed with rabid Groovie fans . . . Also present were zealous new punk rockers, with no use for anything this rooted in tradition.'

The Roundhouse bill saw the Ramones sandwiched between the Groovies and an 'upstart English band', the Stranglers, who had emerged from the UK pub rock scene. (Like the Ramones, the Stranglers would find themselves

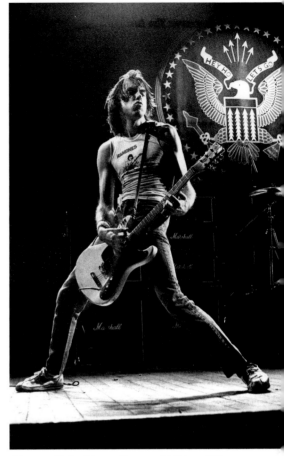

Johnny avoids the phlegm at Hammersmith Odeon, 1980.

associated with punk rock more through accident than design.) The show was originally planned as the first night of a European tour, scuppered when continental promoters withdrew at the last minute and almost caused the cancellation of their two London dates. To coincide with the visit, a single featuring two cuts from the debut album, 'Blitzkrieg Bop' backed by 'Havana Affair', was scheduled for UK release on 9 July.

The 2,000-strong crowd at Chalk Farm was a massive leap in terms of the Ramones' audience size. But, booked into a Shepherds Bush bed-and-breakfast hotel, they endured the lack of air conditioning, vintage sandwiches and warm beer their neophyte status afforded them.

As Dee Dee recalled, 'Our first look at London consisted of walking around Hyde Park at four in the morning. It was very low budget stuff. That's how Danny [Fields] showed us around town.'

Once the group and crew reached the Roundhouse, the atmosphere of overheated ennui evaporated as the level of interest became obvious. There were 'sold out' signs, and, after their soundcheck, a steady procession of London's punk elite came backstage to meet the band.

As Fields recalls, 'These cool-looking guys were hanging around. They said they were a band calling themselves the Clash, but that they were still just rehearsing and didn't feel they were virtuosic enough to play in public. "Are you kidding?" said Johnny. "I hope you're coming tonight. We're lousy. We can't play. If you wait until you can play, you'll be too old to get up there. We stink, really. But it's great."'

Sex Pistol Johnny Rotten and his punk sidekick Sid Vicious also swung by. 'Johnny Rotten asked me if he could come through the back door and meet the band,' recalls Arturo Vega. 'He asked me, "If they don't like me will they beat me up?" He thought the Ramones were a real gang.' In what was to become a Ramones tradition, an unusually nervous Rotten was handed a beer. As Dee Dee revealed, 'The Ramones always put a few drops of piss in anything they give their guests as a little joke.'

Vicious was completely in awe of Dee Dee, and followed him around like a needy puppy. Dee Dee was proabably not the best role model the impressionable and naïve Sidney could have chosen. The future Pistol took to dressing like his idol, and later took up the bass – which he learnt by shooting speed and playing along to *Ramones*.

Whatever they were expecting, we gave them. We totally freaked them out. *Joey Ramone*

Vicious also developed an unhealthy interest in smack (once famously filling his syringe from a toilet bowl) and professional groupies that was to backfire tragically. 'Sid was just an imitator,' Vega recounts, 'he started wearing that chain with the padlock because Dee Dee was wearing one.'

'He really looked up to me, and he loved the Ramones, and that caused him a lot of grief,' concurred Dee Dee. But the show itself introduced the enthusiastic crowd to the Ramones' accelerated live set. It also introduced the band to the peculiarly British custom of spitting at bands. It took them completely by surprise, according to Flamin' Groovie Chris Wilson: 'When they came off, Johnny Ramone was in floods of tears because the punks had been spitting on the band. That was a purely London thing – nobody did that in New York. I remember him saying, "They got it on my guitar . . . they got it on my pick!" And Joey still didn't know if they'd gone down well or not. "Did they like us? Did they hate us?" He really couldn't tell.'

The following night saw the Ramones in the more familiar environment of a small club. Once again supporting the Flamin' Groovies, they played Dingwalls at Camden Lock. Like the previous night's gig, the show was a sell out and the Ramones were visited by many who defined punk in the UK. Members of the Clash (due to make their public debut supporting the Pistols on the same day as the Roundhouse gig) and the Pistols were in attendance alongside future Damned, Generation X, Chelsea and Pretenders personnel.

Despite their personal pilgrimage, Joey was not unduly impressed with the Sex Pistols: 'They were a creation of Malcolm McLaren's genius, a good way to sell sweaters at the Sex boutique, you know what I mean? Sell bondage gear and stuff. We thought

'Fiercely retarded' – Johnny and Joey, 1977.

they were cool too, but they weren't real. They were like a figment of Malcolm's imagination and they made him a lot of money.'

Also at the show was Mark Perry, a nineteen-year-old bank clerk later to become the voice of the punk revolution through his fanzine – the Ramonically-titled *Sniffin' Glue*. As with John Holmstrom in the States, the impact of the Ramones on Perry inspired a seminal publication. As he recalls, 'The first I heard about the punk rock movement is reading about the New York scene . . . Then the Ramones album came out, first album and it was on import . . . I was just blown away. It was like . . . fucking hell, what an exciting album! . . . This was something special, their whole attitude. It was the Ramones coming over was why I decided to do the fanzine.'

First published on 13 July 1976, *Sniffin' Glue* was the first of what became an avalanche of British punk fanzines. Cheaply produced, often photocopied on works premises out of office hours, these publications documented the birth of the movement from street level. Before folding in September 1977, after fourteen issues, *Sniffin' Glue* hit the first waves of punk rock long before the whole scene became beached on its own dogma. And the Ramones had set the ball rolling.

The British music press reacted with ambivalence to the band's brief stopover. In *Melody Maker*, Allan Jones threw around phrases like 'fiercely retarded' and 'violently expressed nihilism', while *NME*'s Max Bell could see the inherent humour of the Ramones: 'Closer to a comedy routine than a band . . . the guys on the mixer hated them and they hate the guys on the mixer back. I laughed solidly for half an hour . . . The appeal is purely negative, based on their not being able to play a shit or give a shit . . . imbecilic adolescent ditties but still oodles more exciting than the majority of bands.' In *Zigzag*, Kris Needs approved of how 'the Ramones gig was the high powered rock cartoon we had expected, and very enjoyable too.'

The first issue of *Sniffin' Glue* opened with Mark Perry's unequivocally positive review: 'The ol' Roundhouse just reeked of glue last Sunday night. The Ramones, armed with miniature baseball bats beat the hell out of all contenders for the "most exciting band of the year" stakes. The Groovies failed because they stuck too rigidly to the Beatles/*Thank Your Lucky Stars* format but the Ramones blasted out non-stop. It was all modern and hard.'

I really feel England and Europe are for the most part really on top of things, they see things realistically, they hit the nail on the head. Certain people in America saw it too, y'know, but not enough. *Joey Ramone*

This spectrum of reaction, from incomprehension to unconditional enthusiasm, was becoming the norm. In a much later piece, the *NME*'s Matt Snow contextulised the impact and significance of the show: 'First time in the UK, the Ramones ambled on stage, mouthed "One-too-freefour!" and piled straight into "Blitzkrieg Bop". Halfway through, about five seconds later, they twigged the sound had packed up, and stalked off cursing, returning moments later to play their entire repertoire in 30 hell-for-leather minutes. None of us had ever seen anything like it – and when Dee Dee split his thumb open on a bass string, spurting blood all over his white Fender Precision and Prince Charles T-shirt, we knew the Ramones were rock 'n' roll maniacs in the grand old style.'

The impact of the Ramones' kinetic performance garnered publicity out of all proportion to their popularity. In many respects, Britain was a much more favourable environment than the USA for a new band to become well-known in a relatively short time. The immense size of the US was an obstacle to national coverage, whereas the UK provided a more intensive hothouse in which both the Ramones and punk could germinate. John Peel's 10 p.m. weekday programme on BBC Radio One provided new bands with a national showcase, while American radio was organised regionally, with non-mainstream music relegated to marginal niche slots.

UK punk audiences were also younger and more enthusiastic than their US counterparts, which led to a faster assimilation of the subculture. Although the British scene was centred around London, within months there was a punk rocker on every high street – in the US, New York (and later, Los Angeles) provided the focal point. You didn't find punks in Nebraska or Tennessee.

Johnny brings New York punk to the European mainland, 1977.

As Caroline Coon observed in *Melody Maker*, 'While New York cultivates avant-garde and intellectual punks like Patti Smith and Television, the British teenager, needing and being that much more alienated from rock than America ever was, has little time for such aesthetic requirements. British punk rock is emerging as a fierce, aggressive-destructive onslaught. There's an age difference, too. New York punks are mostly in their mid-twenties. The members of the new British punk bands squirm if they have to tell you they are over eighteen.'

Within weeks of the Ramones touching down in the UK, the music press ran letters from old rockers, decrying the perceived lack of musicality, while other correspondents welcomed the shift away from mass-marketed 'big-screen' rock. On 21 July, however, the *NME* published a letter from a frustrated wanna-be rock journalist. 'The Ramones are the latest bumptious band of degenerate no-talents whose most notable achievement

Joey vs. the microphone, 1977.

to date is their ability to advance beyond the boundaries of New York City . . . purely on the strength of a spate of convincing literature . . . the Ramones have gotten from the underground press since their triumphant Roundhouse concert,' he sneered, calling them 'notoriously discordant'. 'The New York Dolls and Patti Smith have proved that there is some life pumping away in the swamps and gutters of New York and they are the only acts which originated from the N.Y. club scene worthy of any praise. The Ramones have absolutely nothing at all that is of relevance or importance and should be rightly filed and forgotten.' This stream of invective and prejudice, masquerading as hipness, was penned by future Smiths miserabilist Steven Morrissey.

As *Punk*'s Mary Harron observed, 'I felt that what we had done as a joke in New York had been taken for real in England by a younger and more violent audience . . . What to me had been a much more adult and intellectual bohemian rock culture in New York became this crazy teenage thing in England.'

I think Malcolm took a lot of elements of the New York scene and transplanted them to London. *John Holmstrom*

The British audience adapted the look and attitude that had existed for the past couple of years in the New York punk scene. The difference between the initial rush of British bands and the Ramones is that the Clash, the Damned, et al had a knowing perception of 'punk' in a way that the Ramones could not possibly have.

The Ramones had not set out to be a 'punk band' in the way so many later groups would. Essentially, Da Brudders had distilled a diverse set of influences into the ferocious template that would become 'punk'. The UK media soon seized upon the Sex Pistols as the icons of the movement, the sensationalist press viewing punk as a kind of extreme cultural perversion. British youth subculture had already set in place a tradition whereby punks simply followed on from teddy boys, rockers, mods, hippies and skinheads. In the tabloid consciousness, punk was measured in degrees of extremity. While the Ramones were musically radical, their image was a pure distillation of rock 'n' roll. The Sex Pistols, on the other hand, were singing about anarchy, the monarchy, and abortions. They gave Fleet Street a raging hard-on in a way that 'Rockaway Beach' couldn't hope to compete with.

The period immediately following the Ramones' UK debut was one of intense activity on the punk scene. The Damned and the Buzzcocks played their first live gigs, while the Clash continued rehearsing and playing for friends. Such diverse acts as Alternative TV, Wire, Chelsea, Eater and Subway Sect formed during the summer.

With the Ramones back in the States, the Sex Pistols became the media's focal point. McLaren's media savvy ensured his band were at the centre of a maelstrom of hype and opprobrium. Described by Charles Shaar Murray in *NME* as 'a different cup of manic

monomania than the Ramones', the Pistols were already garnering attention from a number of record labels. However, McLaren's game plan called for more than a street-level buzz. The quickest route to mass exposure was by exploiting the media's tendency toward hysteria.

The attitude of the American press was less neurotic – as McLaren had discovered, when his attempts to promote the New York Dolls as communists in red leather failed to attract attention. Right on cue, however, the Ramones found themselves distantly embroiled in a typically British controversy.

Labour backbench MP James Dempsey, Honourable Member of Parliament for Coatbridge, Scotland, claimed a link between the lyrics of 'Now I Wanna Sniff Some Glue' and the deaths of some teenage solvent abusers in his constituency. (The deaths occurred prior to the release of *Ramones*.) He informed the *Glasgow Evening Times* of his plan to propose a bill prohibiting the sale of glue to minors, which ultimately never found its way on to the statute books.

Whereas Malcolm McLaren would have fanned the flames of this parochial furore, Joey simply pointed out the blindingly obvious: 'I hope that everyone understands that the song is a joke, we know the stuff is dangerous . . . you always feel sick afterwards.'

The keenness of British politicians to weigh in with their views on punk rock was matched only by the speed at which punks embraced a political agenda. Much of this took the form of posturing. While Joe Strummer of the Clash was undoubtedly a progressive thinker, Steve Jones of the Sex Pistols played along with McLaren's P. T. Barnum approach to anarchism. As he was happy to admit, 'we was only in it for the piss up and the birds after the show.'

Whereas the Pistols played with politics as shock theatre, the Clash seemed committed to the brand of grassroots socialism that infused many of their lyrics. The Buzzcocks, with their Ramonic buzzsaw guitars and more personal lyrics, were primarily concerned with sexual politics. This politicised approach led sections of the press and audience to judge bands by their political attitudes, as well as the way they looked and sounded. Those whose agendas survived scrutiny were deemed to have 'street credibility'. Bands with no political or social agenda were not to be taken seriously – like the Damned, or, indeed, the Ramones.

In classic pose in England, 1977 (Johnny, Tommy, Joey, Dee Dee).

Where's da bus . . . ? (Dee Dee, Joey, Tommy, Johnny) 1977.

Playing With The Art School Boys

The music scene changed for the better when the punk movement exploded. It changed everything. Clothing, fashion, magazines. It was a street thing. And the designers picked up on it. It's pure American. It's from the guts.

Joey Ramone

While the British punk scene was coalescing around the 100 Club Festival in September 1976, the Ramones had just completed their first American tour. The band had played in Los Angeles and San Francisco for the first time, and were preparing for two dates at the New Yorker theatre in Toronto, before heading back to Long Island for a couple of shows with Talking Heads.

It was all a comedown after the enthusiasm of the punk audience in London – the Long Island gigs marred by urban rednecks, who came to batter anybody who looked like a punk rocker. Joey wrote the wistful 'Swallow My Pride' as a reflection on the band's return from the UK. As Legs McNeil recounted in *Please Kill Me*:

'Joey kept saying "Legs, you wouldn't believe it! . . . They love it!" I had no idea of what he was talking about, because at that time, punk was just the magazine, the Ramones, Richard Hell, Johnny Thunders, Patti Smith and the Dictators . . . So when Joey told me that the Roundhouse gig went well, I was like "Great, I'm glad, but what's England got to do with punk? I mean, when's America gonna like us?"'

Almost by way of a response, *Los Angeles Times* critic Robert Hilburn attacked the band's emphasis on simplicity: 'The songs are too short . . . the lyrics are dismal; the musicianship is rarely above that of the average garage band and the relentless tempo and tone show almost no variation.' The hippie reviewer at the *San Francisco Examiner* was similarly less than delighted: 'Just when we've found the answer to swine flu, along comes the Ramones.'

Audience response was several steps ahead of the pundits, especially in L.A. As Joey explained, 'It was the closest thing to the UK, where the band was huge.' As with punk rock in London, the Ramones' performances in L.A. sowed the seeds of the hardcore scene that would develop on the West Coast by the end of the decade. 'They were waiting for us, the kids were hungry, really excited by the band, [the L.A. gigs were] the first tidal wave, the tsunami that washed away all the bullshit. It helped rid the Earth of the old debris.' (The Ramones' second show at L.A.'s Roxy was recorded, recently reissued by Rhino/Warner as part of their excellent repackaging of *Leave Home*.)

Although 'Blitzkrieg Bop' would latterly be recognised as one of the Ramones' classics, it had sunk like a stone so far as the *Billboard* chart was concerned. The punk label was proving as much of a handicap in the US as it had been an advantage in Britain. It was decided that a softer approach was necessary. The jagged edges of Da Brudders were reduced to soft focus with the US-only release of 'I Wanna Be Your Boyfriend'. In the misguided hope that impressionable young girls would mistake the Ramones for the Bay City Rollers, Sire commissioned a sleeve that pictured the band in a manner Tommy described as 'dreamy and not too threatening'. But no one was fooled, and the single failed to chart. The conundrum of being seen as the epitome of punk rock, while striving for mass exposure, would bedevil the band throughout their career. Johnny adopted a typically stoic attitude to it: 'Whaddya gonna do? We don't care if they wanna call us dat. It doesn't matter one way or the other.'

We didn't blow our best fourteen songs on the first album and come back with a weaker second one – which is what always happens with bands. *Johnny Ramone*

The Ramones' live set comprised more than double the number of songs featured on their debut album. It ensured they could sidestep the compositional problems associated with that difficult second album. As Tommy explained, 'we recorded them in the order they were written; we wanted to show a slight progression in song structure.'

Toward the end of October, the Ramones checked into the Sundragon Studios, a converted eighth-floor loft on 21st Street and Fifth Avenue. 'It was built like a home studio,' Tommy recalls, 'sixteen tracks, state-of-the-art 1976 with Studor tape recorders from Switzerland.'

With *Ramones* producer Craig Leon having left Sire, the production job was handed to Tony Bongiovi who had previously worked for Motown, as well as at the Record Plant – where he'd encountered Tommy during the production of Jimi Hendrix's *Band of Gypsys* album. Bongiovi delegated wisely, sharing production duties with Tommy and bringing in Ed Stasium as engineer.

Stasium had worked with Bongiovi for three years at the Venture Sound studio, before moving to Canada in 1975. Looking back on his introduction to the band, he recalls, 'I had never heard of the Ramones. . . I very rapidly acclimated, like, "Oh, this is really cool. This is what I used to do when I was fourteen or fifteen years old – just bang on a guitar, turn up the amp, and whack it out."'

The engineer had also caught the band in action at CBGB's in September. 'It was

sweaty, stinky rock 'n' roll to the max and it was great,' he enthused. 'I couldn't understand where everybody had come from. It was a whole new world.'

But his newfound association with the Ramones also entailed disappointment: 'I actually thought I was producing that record. I was very shocked when I got *Leave Home* back
and the credit read, "Tony Bongiovi & T. Erdelyi." [Bongiovi said,] "They must've forgot
ya, Eddy. Don't worry, we'll get you next time." And I think they misspelled my name.'

I'd love to see a real geek . . . a real one. *Dee Dee Ramone*

Described by Tommy as 'happy pop, less arty, with more real musicianship,' *Leave
Home* was recorded quickly and cheaply, costing only slightly more than $10,000.
Although still a meagre budget, there is a discernible improvement in sound quality. 'We
had a better studio,' confirms Tommy, 'with better engineers and we also had more time.'

Regardless of such refinements, Bongiovi acclaimed *Leave Home* as 'a grinding wall
of sound'. The production process continued the emphasis on simplicity that was the
band's motif. As Stasium recalls, 'For *Leave Home* they set up to track, we did three
songs, and then the rest the next day. It was really quick. We just basically double-
tracked the guitars and put Joey's voice on, maybe a little percussion.' As with *Ramones*,
Johnny played no solos, although Stasium provided additional guitar on 'Sheena Is A

Punk Rocker' and a smatter-
ing of backing vocals elsewhere. At slightly over half an
hour in duration, the album
was once again succinct
enough not to impose on the
shortest attention span.

While the band may have
edged forward in a technolog-
ical sense, in terms of content
the new album trod a familiar
path. 'Pinhead' – its 'gabba
gabba, hey!' chorus inspired
by the 'gabba gabba, she is
one of us' chant in Tod
Browning's 1932 cinematic
nightmare, *Freaks* – rivalled
'Blitzkrieg Bop' for ram-a-
lama chantabilty. 'Suzy Is A
Headbanger' paralleled 'Judy
Is A Punk'. 'California Sun'

Leave Home – the not-at-all-difficult second album.

evoked the band's fascination with the surf sound, in the manner of 'Let's Dance'. 'You Should Never Have Opened That Door' occupied much the same horror-movie territory as 'I Don't Wanna Go Down To The Basement', and Dee Dee aired his military fixation again on 'Commando'. ('They get them ready for Viet Nam/From old Hanoi to East Berlin.')

There was, however, a marked increase in saccharine content, with the inclusion of more reflective numbers written by Joey. 'I Remember You', 'Oh Oh I Love Her So', 'Swallow My Pride' and 'What's Your Game?' provided respite from the kinetic dementia of 'Gimme Gimme Shock Treatment', 'Now I Wanna Be A Good Boy' and 'You're Gonna Kill That Girl'.

Like a biker stripping down a Harley-Davidson, they've removed the arrangement, the harmonies, the twenty-piece orchestras, the introductions, the coda, and even the melody. They've stripped down the Spector sound, unravelled it until all that remains is a single scarcely recognisable thread. *Mick Farren,* NME

Identified by John Holmstrom as the album's 'hit', 'Carbona Not Glue' was a blisteringly infectious number about solvent abuse which, once again, produced a minor moral panic. The song extolled the virtues of Carbona cleaning fluid over 'shooting glue', and had to be removed from the album to prevent a lawsuit for unlicensed use of a trademark.

Those who couldn't see the humour in the lyric may just have been dumb enough to lose sleep over kids shooting up with solvents. 'It's absurd, like saying you should try something more poisonous,' explained Tommy. Subsequent pressings of *Leave Home* replaced 'Carbona' with a version of the less troublesome 'Sheena' recorded after the album sessions, or, in the UK, 'Babysitter'.

With the album scheduled for release on 10 January, Joey saw out 1976 nursing an ankle infection that necessitated an operation – which in turn cancelled two festive shows at CBGB's and a New Year's Eve gig in L.A. A proposed tour of the UK with the Sex Pistols had also fallen through, as there was no time for advance promotion.

Irrespective of these setbacks, the Ramones approached punk's *annus mirabilis* in good shape. Interviews in *Creem* and coverage in *Billboard* had raised the band's profile outside of their home turf. *Ramones* regularly featured on end-of-year lists in the music press, and the growth of punk in Britain guaranteed *Leave Home* was eagerly anticipated there.

Stateside too, the critics sometimes lavished glowing praise. In *Rolling Stone*, Ken Tucker led the way : 'They have lost none of their intensity, and if to "leave home" implies a certain broadening of experience, its main evidence on the new record is an occasional use of harmony and the boys' discovery of Carbona, a substitute for airplane glue in getting high . . . The Ramones make rousing music and damn good jokes, but they're in a bind: the hard rock of this group is so pure it may be perceived as a freak novelty by an awful lot of people.'

UK ad for **Leave Home,** *referencing the Roundhouse gigs.*

Still rooting for his homeboys, *Village Voice*'s Robert Christgau had little time for those who didn't 'get' Da Brudders: 'People who consider this a one-joke act aren't going to change their minds now. People who love the joke for its power, wit, and economy will be happy to hear it twice.'

Back in Britain, the media was focusing on the re-enactment of wartime *bonhomie*, for the Queen's Silver Jubilee celebrations. In the real world, much of the populace was preoccupied with rising unemployment and inflation. A climate of enforced boredom and worsening social conditions provided the manure in which UK punk took root.

Although the Damned made it onto vinyl first with the Stooges-influenced 'New Rose', the Sex Pistols' epoch-defining 'Anarchy in the UK' had created the sort of moral shitstorm Malcolm McLaren dreamed of. Their controversial appearance on the *Today* TV programme, and the subsequent cancellation of much of their national tour, was worth its weight in newsprint.

Punk had been given form by Fleet Street: it was the ugly face of youth, awash in its own bodily fluids, and bent on insurrection. They'd even stuck safety pins through Her Majesty's flag. Art-school political theorising shared column inches with tips on how to organise your own royalist street party, and the nation seemed under siege from its young.

What actually happened was that a pantheon of bands had emerged from a maelstrom of activity part-inspired by the Ramones. The music press had constructed a punk hierarchy, with Da Brudders installed as founding fathers. Unsurprisingly, the new

The Ramones' classic front line; Dee Dee, Joey and Johnny in 1977.

album was acclaimed as 'magnificent' (*NME*), and, in an expansive eight-page piece on N.Y. punk in *Zigzag*, Kris Needs enthused, 'The Ramones have burst into 1977 with a follow up every bit as good, and possibly better, than its predecessor.' Once again, the level of foreign interest far exceeded the attention they were receiving in their homeland, where the album peaked at number 148 on the *Billboard* chart.

After warming up with some dates at CBGB's in February (the second of which took place on the same night they supported Blue Oyster Cult), the Ramones set off on the first of the marathon tours for which they were to become known. Beginning with a five-night residency at the Whiskey in L.A., the band undertook a further 30 dates in the next two months that saw them zig-zagging across the US.

'We would go everywhere in our van,' reminisced Dee Dee. 'We'd drive back and forth, back and forth, across the country with the van, with about fourteen people in it. We could always tell when a person was a musician by their pained, hunchback type walk when they just got out of the van.'

As well as storing up orthopaedic problems for later life, the band delivered blistering sets to mostly enthusiastic crowds. Support spots with the Kinks, Toto and Peter Frampton offered them the opportunity to freak out the older generation, while Lou

Reed, Iggy Pop and Phil Spector came to check out the Ramones. Spector was so impressed that he invited them to visit his home – a bloodless encounter that laid the ground for their 1980 collaboration, *End Of The Century.*

As with the Ramones' first visit to the UK, the tour was a catalyst that motivated young punks to form bands. One such was Jello Biafra, the future Dead Kennedys front-man, respected political activist, and candidate for Mayor of San Francisco. 'When Johnny hit the first chord,' testifies Biafra, 'the ten of us in the front row who knew who the Ramones were, knew that this was going to be much more extreme than the records gave us any right to expect. For the next 20-40 minutes, the Ramones mowed down everybody in the room. It totally blew me away, in part because I kept turning around and seeing the looks of shock and horror on people's faces.'

Four days after a homecoming date at CBGB's with the Cramps, the Ramones set off for Europe backed by Talking Heads. Their first continental tour began in Zurich, followed by shows in France, Belgium, Holland, Denmark, Sweden, Finland, and a return to Britain.

Unlike the flying visit ten months earlier, they played seventeen dates from Glasgow to Penzance. When they kicked off in Liverpool on 19 May, Joey and Dee Dee were par-ticularly excited about visiting the 'Birthplace of the Beatles'™. *NME*'s Julie Burchill took a more idiosyncratic viewpoint, describing Joey as 'much more of a Beatle than Lennon ever was'.

This ain't a Wittgenstein tutorial, this is rock 'n' roll. *Julie Burchill*

Unlike London, there was no *prêt-a-porter* punk scene in Liverpool waiting to greet the Ramones. 'I was surprised at how empty [the gig venue] Eric's was,' reported Burchill, 'and those present were definitely not the breed detected at London new music gigs; I saw just one girl in rubber [who could well have been Joey's girlfriend, who'd taken to wearing a rubber dress complete with simulated armpit hair]. Otherwise flares were the order of the day – but a Bored Teenager is a Bored Teenager, no matter the diameter of his trousers.'

Although it was true that punk hadn't touched Liverpool in the same way it had Manchester, the less fashion-conscious crowd was emblematic of the Ramones. As Linda Stein observed, 'You could spot our audience from the street. They didn't have safety pins in their ears, they didn't have spiked hair, they didn't have the military look. They looked like kids in their denim and long hair, and maybe a motorcycle jacket if they could afford one.'

Essentially, although the Ramones were the godfathers of punk, the dirty rock 'n' roll at the core of their music engaged the unpretentious kids who'd otherwise be rocking to Slade or Status Quo.

The tour's breakneck schedule allowed little time for sightseeing or reflection. Whereas the Talking Heads avidly consumed European culture and cuisine, Da

Brudders only became keen on visiting Paris once they discovered the city boasted a McDonalds. In England, the band subsisted almost exclusively on Indian food – later inspiring the lines 'Hanging out on Second Avenue / Eating chicken vindaloo' on 'I Just Want To Have Something To Do'.

The obvious differences between the bourgeois, educated Heads and their headliners caused some friction on the road. 'The Ramones were punks on the street, and the Talking Heads were collegiate intellectuals. They were entire opposites on the spectrum,' observed Ed Stasium. But the two bands were lumped together on account of being signed by Sire, though they shared few common musical reference points.

'They didn't like the Talking Heads because it was "art music",' explained Seymour Stein. 'They liked Blondie, but they *really* hated everyone, including me and especially each other.'

Such negativity on the part of Joey, Johnny, Dee Dee and Tommy was partly artifice, based on a punk attitude and the fact that brudders habitually squabble. More significantly, it was also due to disparate personalities grating on each other in close confinement. The crappy food, transport and accommodation, allied to the demands of playing most nights of the week, meant that periods of bitching and sulking inevitably ensued.

It takes a long time for things to spread in the United States. It spreads from New York to California, but misses the whole middle. *Johnny Ramone*

Johnny – with his fines for lateness, insistence on listening to baseball games, and stern demeanour – wasn't exactly a barrel of laughs for the rest of the band, who caricatured him as a tyrant. Dee Dee was generally pissed off about having to stay straight on the road, prone to whining and depression. Joey found the experience physically gruelling, while Tommy would have been happier back in the studio. What kept them together was a determination to succeed, and the fact that, aside from Tommy, they didn't have a lot of alternative options. So they just kept going.

'They were sort of within themselves,' recalls Danny Fields. 'I remember a long car ride and occasionally someone would say something, but mostly they'd look out of the window.'

The Ramones completed their UK tour in London on 6 June, supported by the Heads and Australian proto-punks the Saints. Two days later they were back at CBGB's with the Cramps, and within another week had embarked on another tortuous schedule – beginning in Toronto, before heading across the USA for the second time in six months.

This relentless gigging was consistent with the breakneck pace of their live set. The metaphor became concrete, when the promoter of a show in Madison, Wisconsin withheld the group's $450 share of takings when he felt they hadn't played long enough. The tour continued throughout July, finishing at the Whiskey on 10 August – the same L.A. venue where the trek began, six months earlier.

Tommy outside Eric's in Liverpool, 1977.

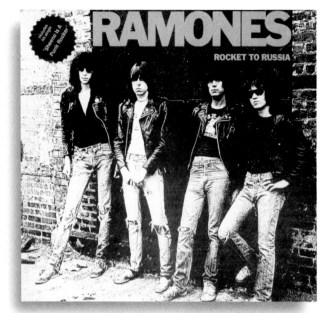

Rocket To Russia – *the Ramones' third album was rated by many fans as Da Brudders' finest.*

Having circled much of America and Europe under their own steam, Fields and Stein felt the band would gain access to more prestigious bills if they signed to a major bookings agency. 'Critics were going nuts, but we still had a hard time breaking into concerts – where Aerosmith and KISS were the rule,' explained Johnny.

The management enlisted the well-established Premier talent agency to handle the group. Premier assigned Tim McGrath as the Ramones' agent, who quickly established a low-rent way of gaining nationwide exposure: 'We'd hit different parts of the country – like for the West Coast, they'd go out and do eleven shows in fourteen days, keep the costs down and then fly home. Or they'd go from Texas to Florida and then come home. Another peculiarity was that if they were within a two hundred mile radius of home, they'd come home every night. That saved a lot of money over the years in hotel bills.'

While Premier were lining up some more van mileage, a gap in the touring schedule sent them scuttling into midtown New York's Media Sound studio to begin their third album. Although the Sire contract required one album a year, as far as Johnny was concerned time was money – and the more records released, the greater the possibility of scoring a hit.

'Swallow My Pride' and 'Sheena Is A Punk Rocker' had been released as singles on both sides of the Atlantic. The gentle 'Swallow My Pride' sank without trace, but 'Sheena' climbed to number 81 in the *Billboard* chart and enjoyed far higher placings in Europe. 'I played it for Seymour Stein,' Joey remembered, 'he flipped out and said, "We gotta record that song now." It was like back in the Fifties; you'd rush into the studio because you thought you had a hit, then put it right out. To me, "Sheena" was the first surf/punk rock/teenage rebellion song.'

The band had seen the Sex Pistols denied the UK number one spot for 'God Save The Queen', on account of some sharp practice in reporting sales figures that week. But Johnny was particularly vexed to see a group who trailed in the Ramones' sonic slipstream overtaking them in terms of sales and publicity. 'I remember Johnny bringing in "God Save The Queen",' Ed Stasium revealed. 'He said, "These guys copied us, and we want to sound better than this."'

'You have to remember that the focus was always on singles,' explained Legs McNeil, 'as in "hit singles". Don't kid yourselves – even though the Ramones were the hippest and the coolest, and they really did start punk rock, they were still always looking for that elusive Top Ten.'

Johnny concurred, 'We came first. We did what came naturally to us. A lot of bands have just copied us and they are not being themselves.'

The new album, *Rocket To Russia*, maintained the Bongiovi/Stasium/Erdelyi production team that presided over *Leave Home*. Originally entitled *Get Well*, the album title was drawn from a song-in-progress that evolved into 'Ramona'.

The word minimalism gets bandied about with the Ramones. But, 'I Don't Care' – how much more basic can you get? It's truth, wrapped up in a very simple package. *Tommy Ramone*

'They wanted to start making more of a production number out of it,' confirms Stasium. Although the album was quickly produced (it was in the shops inside ten weeks), costs escalated to around $30,000. Such an amount was small potatoes by Toto standards, but indicated the band's desire to achieve 'the hit'.

Producer Bongiovi had invested the profits from his work on Meco's *Star Wars Theme* disco cash-in to build his own studio, the Power Station. Construction was still in progress while *Rocket To Russia* was being mixed, and there was little in the way of studio effects. Such Spartan conditions necessitated using an external metal stairwell as a reverb chamber. Still, extra guitars were overdubbed by Stasium and Johnny's sound was cleaned up to give it a more radio-friendly quality.

Almost shockingly, a guitar solo was incorporated into 'Here Today, Gone Tomorrow'. But Johnny was still not in the business of prevaricating. 'It's best to do it quickly,' he asserted. 'If the engineer said a take was good, we'd go on to the next one. You don't want to sit there and bullshit – it's your money they're spending.'

The content of *Rocket To Russia* was, once again, similar to its predecessors. But it marked the point at which the Ramones exhausted all material pre-dating their first

Punk *magazine's John Holmstrom illustrated the back cover of* **Rocket To Russia.**

album. The band had been playing 'I Don't Care' and 'Here Today, Gone Tomorrow' since recording their first demo, and many of the other ten originals had been written on the road or during sessions for the previous albums.

Rocket provided a host of durable tub-thumpers to add to their live set: 'Cretin Hop', 'Rockaway Beach', 'We're A Happy Family', 'Teenage Lobotomy'. All were infused with twisted humour and dynamism. 'If there is a greatest Ramones song that I recorded, it's "Teenage Lobotomy",' Stasium announced. 'It's a mini-Ramones symphony. It has every element of what's great about them, in one song: The big drum intro and the "Lobotomy" chant; the little background-harmony ooooohs; the subject matter.'

The band lampooned their way through a minefield of bad taste, exploiting disability, dysfunctional families, drug dealing, homosexuality and mental illness. 'If they want to make themselves more secure by thinking it's *Tom and Jerry*, let them,' snarled Johnny, regarding the cartoon label as a millstone. 'It's an easy cop-out taking shock treatment and lobotomies and stuff lightly. We're just very mean, angry people you know. We're the real thing.'

It takes more than bad playing to make a good punk band. You've got to be talented and genuine, like us. *Tommy Ramone*

'Whenever I'd read that we were a cartoon it really upset me,' added Joey. 'I remember doing an interview on the phone with a guy who said, "You're like cartoon characters." I got really pissed off and said, "What d'ya mean by that?" He said that we had very definite, distinguished personalities. So I didn't mind. If that's what it meant.'

'One thing that people don't realise about the Ramones is that we try to do as much as possible naturally,' Tommy continued. 'We don't force ourselves to do things that don't come naturally to us. That's why it works. No one who's ever listened to us or seen us can call us contrived. It's just us.'

Those who couldn't grasp the Ramones' sense of irony wouldn't be able to see past the record's content. Although the lyrics evoked their usual nightmarish cartoon soundscape, they were, as Joey explained, also grounded in experience: '"Cretin Hop" came from when we were in St. Paul, Minnesota. We went some place to eat and there were just these cretins all over the place. And there was a Cretin Avenue, where we drove into the city.'

As John Holmstrom revealed, 'Rockaway Beach', while ostensibly a super-charged surf choon, was perhaps the most sardonic cut on the album: 'Have you ever been to Rockaway Beach? The place is a sewer. The one time I went there with Joey Ramone, there were crowds of vicious girls in bikinis and – I swear – high heels, drinking tallboys of beer out of little brown paper bags, waiting to get into the next fight. Everyone was stoned on Quaaludes and Tuinals, and I witnessed six different fights in half an hour . . .' Rockaway Beach was a favourite haunt of Joey's, and the kind of place where Dee Dee occasionally took his mother.

Elsewhere on *Rocket*, the usual combination of Joey's romanticism ('Locket Love', 'Ramona'), Dee Dee's chemically-propelled mania ('I Wanna Be Well', 'Why Is It Always This Way?') and surf/garage cover versions ('Surfin' Bird', 'Do You Wanna Dance?') held sway. 'Sheena Is A Punk Rocker' was also re-recorded for inclusion, in a superior mix to the single.

Group identity was maintained in the packaging, with Danny Fields providing an angled view of the band and a brick wall, much like Roberta Bayley's definitive picture the previous year. The back cover and inner sleeve were enlivened by John Holmstrom cartoons depicting the Ramones' universe of geeks, cretins and pinheads.

In many ways, *Rocket To Russia* was a distillation of the band's influences and essence. Cited by Johnny as his favourite Ramones disc, Tommy agreed that they were somewhere near their creative peak during the recording: 'When we did *Rocket To Russia*, we were on a roll, in high gear, touring and everything. At that point, we thought we were gonna make it, that we were on the launching pad. Even if it was a little difficult to write the songs, because we had to write 'em in hotel rooms, once we got into the studio with it, we felt we were in control – that we were in our prime.'

The third Ramones album in two years was met with the customary critical acclaim and disappointing sales. In *Rolling Stone*, Dave Marsh was unequivocal in his praise: '*Rocket To Russia* is the best American rock 'n' roll of the year and possibly the funniest rock album ever made. Not that the Ramones are a joke – they're more worthwhile than almost anything that's more self-conscious because they exist in a pure and totally active state. *Rocket* shows substantial progress in the group's sound – it has opened up so that hints of Beach Boys harmonies float among the power chords . . .'

Creem's Billy Altman was equally enthusiastic, acclaiming *Rocket* as 'the best album the Ramones have done – and that's saying a lot.' In Britain, however, reaction was more lukewarm than previously, largely due to the impact of the Sex Pistols' *Never Mind The Bollocks* and the Clash's eponymous debut album. *NME*'s Nick Kent confessed that his reaction

Recorded in December 1977, **It's Alive** *shows the band at their live peak.*

was 'jaded' on account of exposure to *Bollocks*. Over at *Zigzag*, Colin Keinch shared little of the urbane Kent's ennui: 'It's got all the right ingredients – excitement, innocence, pulverising power, great tunes, neat variations in pace, amazing songs and an attitude so dynamic that I challenge even an asleep Bob Harris [laidback hippie presenter of the BBC's *Old Grey Whistle Test*] on Mandrax to keep still while it's playing.'

Promotion for *Rocket To Russia* was assisted by Sire's new distribution deal with Warner. Aided by the limited but significant airplay afforded 'Sheena', and the Ramones' perpetual touring, the album peaked at a healthy number 48 on the *Billboard* chart.

The band immediately returned to the road, spending much of October supporting Iggy Pop. During these dates, they suffered a severe financial blow when all their equipment was stolen along with their truck. It set the Ramones back around $30,000, but failed to prevent them fulfilling a series of headline dates during November.

Another disaster occurred before a concert at the Capitol Theatre in Passaic, New Jersey. As Legs Mc Neil recalls, 'Joey used a tea kettle as a makeshift vaporiser, inhaling the steam to clear his nasal cavities and throat before singing. Unfortunately, something went wrong, and Joey was rushed to the hospital with second and third degree burns.'

The hospital swathed the agonised Joey in cream as a temporary measure – he refused to countenance pulling out of the gig. Despite his burnt skin frying in the cream, which melted under the stage lights, the consummate trouper completed the show. 'It was the bravest performance I've ever seen,' attested Sire publicist Janis Schacht. 'He ended up in New York Hospital Burn Centre for three weeks, not one. His entire throat filled with blisters.'

Joey was still recovering from his injuries when the band headed to England for Christmas and New Year dates. Their wisdom was thrown into question on the first night, when the accident-prone frontman caught his blistered skin on a microphone –peeling off a six-inch-long strip.

Such recklessness was driven by a commitment to the growing legions of Ramones devotees. 'We've always cared about our fans, we always felt they came first,' insisted Joey. 'There's a hunger there and it's satiated by just going out and playing. And also the reaction of your audience, your fans. I mean, to me, that's the ultimate high. Performing is the best therapy in the world.'

The Ramones played ten British dates in fifteen days, culminating with a return to north London's Rainbow theatre on New Year's Eve. Support that night was provided by Generation X and the Rezillos, two bands indicative of the diverse paths that punk was taking. Generation X, fronted by the pretty but vapid Billy Idol, were effectively mods in punk drag, without a great degree of substance beyond spiked-up references to the 'Swinging London' of ten years earlier. The Rezillos provided effervescent day-glo punkabilly, which scored a series of UK hits for Sire. And an enthusiastic crowd trashed the front rows of the all-seated venue. The show was recorded, and constitutes the bulk of the band's first live album, *It's Alive.*

Like *Rocket To Russia, It's Alive* documents the Ramones during a period of sure-footed singularity of purpose. 28 songs are rattled through in slightly less than an hour. The opening three numbers – 'Rockaway Beach', 'Teenage Lobotomy' and 'Blitzkrieg Bop' – run into one another, Dee Dee counting in the next song as the band hit the last chord.

If somebody wanted to know what the Ramones' live peformance was like, *It's Alive* provides an accurate impression. Described by Charles Shaar Murray as 'perfect pop songs, streamlined to the Nth degree, fired at you at perfect velocity with machine gun

We don't want to sit around and get depressed though. Life is a joke. Every time you turn on the radio you hear about a murder and some of them are funny. That's what we sing about. *Johnny Ramone*

precision,' it was undoubtedly the finest live recording of the punk era.

However, Sire were unsure of how well it would sell. They sat on the master tapes for over a year before releasing it as a double album in the UK only, in April 1979. As Tommy later observed, 'When it came out on CD here in the United States, I picked one up and I played it and I was surprised how good it was. I didn't remember it being that good, because I had not heard it for many years.'

It marked the end of a productive year: three albums, three singles (four in the UK), 150 concerts. As the Ramones prepared for a mammoth four-month tour of the US starting January 1978, they had every reason to view the New Year with optimism.

Life's A Gas

It would've been a good thing for music if 'Anarchy' and 'Rockaway Beach' would've been number one hits. It would've been a better world. *Johnny Ramone*

Both Johnny Rotten and Sid Vicious (by now a fully-fledged Sex Pistol, following the ousting of bassist Glen Matlock) had attended the Ramones' 1977 end-of-year concert at the Rainbow. The New Year saw the Pistols crossing the Atlantic in the opposite direction, for an American tour that resulted in their spectacular dissolution.

As he'd previously done with the New York Dolls, manager Malcolm McLaren booked his charges into a series of low-rent venues in the South. No New York or L.A. concerts were scheduled, with a gig at the Winterland in San Francisco being the sole concession.

Having initially been denied entry visas, over ten days in January 1978 the Pistols fulfilled the atavistic fantasies of the media. In a miasma of bitching, brawling, screwing, drinking and drug abuse, the band disintegrated. Rotten quit, while Vicious checked into a New York hospital following a heroin overdose. These events received blanket media coverage on both sides of the Atlantic. While the British music press had seen it all before, in America the Sex Pistols became emblematic of punk rock.

It had an immediate negative effect on the Ramones, at a time when Sire – strengthened by their new distribution arrangement with Warners – were attempting to gain a level of exposure for their investment that might mean chart success.

'When the Sex Pistols broke up in San Francisco, it showed everyone that this punk thing wasn't viable. That they were meant to self-destruct and so what's the point of investing in any of them?' said Danny Fields. 'The whole thing just got out of control and whatever chance the Ramones had to get on the radio based on the merit of the music was then wiped out by the Sex Pistols because it became too hot to handle.'

As a concerned Johnny observed at the time, 'We've had a lot of job rejections. We had a lot of radio stations taking us off and rejecting us. We just had a job offer at Notre Dame with Foreigner, and Notre Dame turned us down. We got pulled off stations . . . It had nothing to do with us. We don't look or act like them [the Pistols]. We weren't out to ruin the music business. There's room for everybody.'

January 7, 1978 U.S. $1.50/Canada 60c 18p

MUSICAL EXPRESS

DAMNED, PERE UBU, OTWAY, ALIMANTADO

DA BRUDDERS
In udder woids The Ramones
Pages 22/23

Although the band were not left wanting for gigs (they were on a mammoth four-month trek around the States), airplay for *Rocket To Russia* and its single, 'Do You Wanna Dance?', evaporated.

Fields was less than enchanted. 'The music industry and its half-witted brother, radio, believed that the punk aesthetic contained within itself the engine of self destruction . . . It was simpler to say of the whole array of musicians and music labelled "punk" that it was a fashion statement coming from London or the equivalent of vomiting on strangers in airports. British puke stole the show, and a lot of great music was buried in its flow.'

'The Sex Pistols didn't help at all,' concurred Joey. 'They were into a negative kind of destruction thing, which scared everybody, and we were always into a positive thing – trying to save rock 'n' roll and put the excitement and fun back into it, instead of drawing it all out like Foreigner and Toto.'

The Ramones were not the only band affected by the negativity that afflicted punk rock. 'The stigma of the word punk is something that could not be absorbed into today's American culture as representing anything remotely positive,' asserted Blondie's Chris Stein. 'That's one of the things that held Blondie back so long.'

All I ever wanted to do was be a rock star since I was four and I saw Elvis on *The Ed Sullivan Show* when they banned the TV station from showing shots of him below the waist. But now we're in it the music business is really aggravating. *Johnny Ramone*

Dee Dee took a more literal-minded view: 'I guess our image paid homage to juvenile delinquency and everybody took us for a bunch of juvenile delinquents.'

As if losing the music industry's goodwill wasn't enough, Tommy announced at this time that he wanted to leave the band. The drummer had always been happier behind a mixing desk than a drum kit, and the Ramones' almost non-stop touring had become unbearable for him.

'I was having a lot of fun, I liked making records and feeling that we improved in each of them,' he testified, 'but I became paranoiac during our tours. I like making albums so I decided only to make records and to quit the life on the road.'

Marky Ramone – new kid on the block, 1978 .

Fortunately, there was no acrimony behind his departure and he would complete the current tour, allowing adequate time for a replacement to be recruited. In fact, Tommy had never seen himself as a drummer. 'The truth of the matter was that my function with the Ramones was as a producer and an organiser,' he reflected. 'My least contribution was as a drummer.'

Dee Dee, in particular, was sorry to see his brudder go. 'For a while I used to live with Tommy in Debbie Harry's apartment. I had to admire how Tommy would place importance on the need for decent, human, rational survival, unlike anyone else in our group of friends. Tommy would go to the store and buy himself some hamburger meat and cook them trying to make himself a meal, and I would be lying on a mattress with half a pint of blackberry brandy, watching him cook.'

The blow of Tommy's resignation was softened by his desire to remain involved with production. However, with an album due and further US and European tours mooted for the second part of 1978, a replacement needed to be found with quickfire Ramonic urgency.

The Ramones viewed themselves as music biz outsiders, part of a unique brudder-hood with their closest aides and fans. Recent events had only served to strengthen their siege mentality. Naturally enough, the field of runners and riders was largely drawn from their Bowery homeboys and the wider punk scene.

Blondie's Clem Burke (on the verge of huge transatlantic success with the *Plastic Letters* album), former New York Doll Jerry Nolan (too druggy) and ex-Pistol Paul Cook (too British) were all considered and rejected. The popular candidate was Richard Hell and the Voidoids' drummer Marc Bell, who was well known to the band and had been around the local scene since 1974.

'We knew Marky because he was the drummer of the Voidoids and we thought he was too jazzy and was wasted in that group,' Johnny explained. 'We didn't want to steal the drummer from another band, but he was much better with us.'

Original artwork by Gus Macdonald. The Ramones took this back to New York City and asked John Holmstrom to redo it with Marky substituted for Tommy.

Happily, Johnny's admiration was reciprocated. 'When the Ramones' first album came out, all the bands around CBGB's were envious,' attested Bell. 'They really were a step above the others . . . the Ramones were New York City. Every group I played with looked like the Ramones, when I heard their first record I knew it was the beginning of something new, I never heard anything like that.'

Dee Dee asked the drummer to come to an audition, but it was little more than token. As Bell recalled, 'Tommy said we'd meet at the rehearsal studio, and ten other drummers were waiting around. I knew they wanted me any-way, but I let the others play out of respect. This was in March 1978. I respected Richard [Hell]'s song writing, but we didn't get along and I wanted to go into this other thing.'

Born on 15 July 1956, the newly re-christened Marky Ramone supplanted Dee Dee as the youngest band member. Born in Brooklyn, the drummer grew up in the tough Flatbush area. Marc's father was a longshoreman with long-held trade union affiliations, while his mother ran the Brooklyn College Music Library. His parents encouraged their son's interest in music, as well as imparting to him the significance of wider issues.

Like his new brudders, Marky was a fan of the Beatles, the Rolling Stones, the Kinks and the Who. Unlike the other Ramones he was engaged with social issues, having attended the 1963 United Nations March on Washington DC with his parents as a child. An admirer of Jimi Hendrix Experience drummer Mitch Mitchell and jazz veter-an Buddy Rich, Marky was proficient enough to record two albums with the progres-sive rock trio Dust while still in high school.

After Dust split in 1972, Bell began securing occasional session work and broadening his musical horizons by checking out the bands of the day. He soon developed a liking for the New York Dolls, and, like Joey (who he first met in 1975), became a face on the local scene. He was recruited as drummer for Wayne County's former backing band, the Back Street Boys, and appeared on the *Max's Kansas City 1976* compilation. Shortly after, he encountered Richard Hell and was invited to join the Voidoids.

Having been officially inducted into the Ramones, Marky then set about learning the band's set as well as their new material. Unfazed by the limited time available, Marky entered rehearsals with Tommy in confidence. Unlike his mentor, Marky had no interest in being anything other than the drummer in the Ramones, and was con-vinced he could improve the band's sound.

'Tommy was okay,' he opined. 'I mean, *Rocket To Russia* was good, but at some point the band needed to be stronger.' By May, the new recruit was deemed ready for active duty, and Tommy

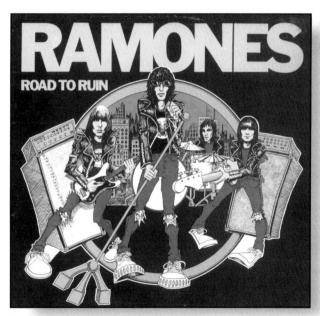

Road To Ruin – *using Gus Macdonald's concept.*

bowed out with a final concert at CBGB's on 4 May. (The gig was a benefit for the Dead Boys' drummer, Johnny Blitz, seriously wounded in a stabbing incident and facing a hefty medical bill.) Although it was fitting that Tommy was playing his swansong on the band's home turf, there was little outpouring of emotion. Within four weeks he was back in Media Sound with the band, as co-producer, with Ed Stasium, on *Road To Ruin*.

Changing drummers made little difference to the anti-punk sentiment of the US music industry. The necessity to make the Ramones more commercially viable had reached boiling point. 'I'm sick of not selling records,' asserted Joey. 'I want to draw more people to the shows, make something happen. If the new album isn't a hit, I'm gonna kill myself.'

It was decided that adjustments to their recording methods were essential, including an unprecedented three-month production period for the new album. It was contrary to Johnny's philosophy of 'do it quick – do it cheap,' but even the band's self-appointed taskmaster was feeling the strain of the relentless tour/album/tour cycle to which the group had yoked themselves.

'At first it was easy,' Johnny opined, 'because we had more time . . . we were doing nothing. We'd just play CBGB's once a month and hang out for four weeks, but now we're on the road. You play every night, you have a day off, you're too tired to write anything . . . We wrote this whole album on the road.'

Tommy was more than content to be ensconced within the control room, which allowed Stasium to add previously unthinkable embellishments to the Ramones sound. 'I really started playing a lot more on *Road To Ruin*. On some of the songs I played everything – even bass . . . I became the fifth member,' he explained. 'Tommy also played some of the guitars on *Road To Ruin* . . . they were writing differently. They started putting little solos in, adding percussion . . . Johnny basically said, "Eddy, you and Tommy finish that stuff up, put some good guitars on, and I'll come and listen to it when you're finished." We did a lot of experimentation on *Road To Ruin*.'

Marky, who was not already worn down by the band's relentless activity, had formed a hedonistic partnership with Dee Dee. As he later recalled, '*Road To Ruin*, you know, getting messed up, not stopping, partying every minute. That's what me and Dee Dee used to do. We partied from morning to night, and after a while it got to him, and it got to me.'

To alleviate pressure, it was decided *Road To Ruin* would contain no more

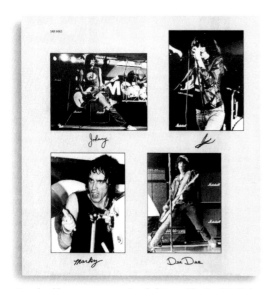

Four brudders, one surname, signed photos on **The Road To Ruin.**

than a dozen songs. 'It was very hard to continue writing fourteen songs an album,' confessed Johnny. 'Everybody else has eight.'

So as not to short-change the fans, a conscious effort was made to extend the running time of individual tracks. It resulted in the band exceeding the half-hour mark for the first time – albeit by little more than a minute.

Despite tampering with the formula, however, *Road To Ruin* hardly heralded a radical departure. But it was certainly softer and sweeter than anything the Ramones had previously recorded, with the acoustic guitars that crept into the mix of *Rocket To Russia* coming to the fore in several songs.

The reduction in raw power emphasised the fragile tenderness of Joey's voice, bringing great sensitivity to 'Questioningly', 'I Just Want To Have Something To Do' and a cover of the Searchers' 'Needles And Pins'. Dee Dee even penned a ballad, 'Don't Come Close', which became the second single to be taken from the disc.

> **_Road To Ruin_ came out on disgusting yellow vinyl. I think I'm the only person who got a red copy.** *Joey Ramone*

More traditionally, the bassist revisited his Germanic influences on the final track, 'It's A Long Way Back'. As with *Rocket To Russia*, a refinement of the Ramones' sound contrasted with some of their lyrics becoming more extreme. Three of the album's songs were set firmly in the psychiatric ward: 'Go Mental', 'Bad Brain' (from which legendary Washington DC reggae/hardcore group Bad Brains took their name) and the album's classic cut, 'I Wanna Be Sedated'.

'That song was about being on the road too long,' explained Joey. 'Getting burned like that [in the NJ tea kettle incident], bits and pieces from different situations, like being on tour in England at Christmas, when everything shuts down: "There's nothing to do, nowhere to go/I wanna be sedated." People didn't use terms like sedated then. This was before Prozac.'

'I Wanna Be Sedated' was eventually released as a single late in 1980, a prime example of the Ramones' wilful mismatching of tune and lyrical content. 'We spent a little time making "Sedated" more produced,' Tommy confessed. 'We were trying to get a single. Which was bittersweet, because we knew it wasn't going to get played with the word sedated in it.'

The album's track listing was rounded off by a series of enjoyable Ramones-lite romps: 'I Wanted Everything', 'I Don't Want You', and the radio-friendly 'She's The One' (issued as a single in the UK in 1979). Side One's closing number, 'I'm Against It', shows the band in characteristic mode – hating absolutely everything, in a lyric containing the album's sole mention of 'geeks'. Equally disappointing for traditionalists, there was no extension of the 'Suzy'/'Judy'/'Sheena' series.

Road To Ruin was released by Sire on 15 September 1978, two days after 'Don't Come Close' was issued as a single. Both were greeted by mixed reviews. *Rolling Stone*'s Charles Young regarded the album as a transitional phase, viewed from a Ramoniac perspective: '*Road To Ruin* is a real good album. It isn't as funny or as powerful as their debut, *Ramones*, but this does not mean the band is losing its grip. It means they figured out that the nigh-pure power chords and satire of their first three records – though enormously satisfying to smart people like myself –was too threatening to dumb people like you.'

In *New York Rocker*, Roy Trakin also saw the need to keep moving or die: '*Road to Ruin* could easily be subtitled *I Just Wanna Improve Myself*. The Ramones are aware that in order to survive they must begin to connect on a personal level, and many of the new songs reflect the positive side of the boys' yin/yang image.'

Dyed-in-the-wool brudder lovers like Robert Christgau filed positive copy, but the

New boy Marky's interest in literature broadens the band's horizons, 1980.

British press took the album as further evidence of the death of punk. The commercial verdict on *Road To Ruin* told a familiar tale – moderate sales in the US, but not enough to impinge on the Top 40, better sales in the UK and Europe. Although it sold in excess of 250,000 copies worldwide, the album failed to provide the Ramones with the mass-market breakthrough they were desperate for. However, as Ed Stasium explained, it still succeeded in finding some new fans: 'People liked *Road To Ruin*. I was talking to Slash of Guns N' Roses once, and he was like, "Dude, that's the best record ever. I learned how to play guitar by listening to *Road To Ruin*."'

Marky Ramone made his live debut as a fully-fledged brudder on 29 June 1978, and was thrust into an epic burst of touring that continued, largely unabated, until May 1979. The Ramones criss-crossed the States, headed up to Toronto (one of Dee Dee's favourite gigs), crossed Northern Europe and visited Ireland for the first time, all ahead of a full British tour. It was followed by yet another American sojourn, during which they passed 1978's 150-gig mark.

People have created images of what we're supposed to be like, they didn't give our personalities a chance. Everybody thinks that the Ramones go on stage smashed out of their heads but we don't even get high before we go on. *Dee Dee Ramone*

Such relentless pursuit of an audience – coupled with the Ramones' traditionally cheapskate travel arrangements, and the *louche* proclivities of a band on the road – hardly provided the gentlest introduction to life as a Ramone. Fortunately, Marky relished touring and quickly adjusted to his new role.

He also discovered that life on the road with the Ramones had little to do with superstars pleasuring groupies with red snappers, or throwing TV sets from hotel windows: 'We were in the tour van once, and we stopped at a restaurant. When our road manager, Monte Melnick, got up to check on the van out in the parking lot, this woman came up to him and said, "Are you taking care of those retarded men?" She thought we were retarded guys in a van, being nursed by Monte. She meant it.'

Having just joined the group, Marky was largely insulated from the frustrations building up within. Joey, Johnny and Dee Dee had been welded together for five solid years, and the strain was starting to show. While Johnny's cost-cutting had undoubtedly served the band well, it had failed to make them rich.

Early in 1979, he revealed that they certainly weren't in it for the money: 'We've been on salary since we started recording. It's not much, it's meagre but it's been okay. When we started it was about $50 a week. Now it's $150 a week – actually that starts next week, a raise from $125. We get $10 a day when we're travelling, and occasionally get a royalty cheque for song writing.'

Rock 'n' Roll High School – *the Ramones go Hollywood . . . almost.*

Johnny's dictatorial tendencies were made worse by the departure of Tommy, who had the organisational experience to wrest control of the band's activities from the guitarist. Once Marky was in the band, Johnny became the group's main decision maker – Joey was incapable of being pushy, just as Dee Dee had an incapacity for remaining straight and lucid.

Although presented as a fraternal democracy, it was decided that only *original* members of the band would have a vote on any issues. The joint songwriting credits remained, a state of affairs that benefited Johnny more than Joey and Dee Dee. Despite such machinations, Danny Fields supported his methods: 'Johnny was very clever, faithful, loyal and honest: he knew exactly what to do and when to do it. Johnny Ramone couldn't stand mistakes or stupidity, so sometimes he was rude with us, but he never was so without a good reason. He had a diary of all concerts, so he knew exactly where they had been and how many people went to see them. He was very precise.'

As the disenfranchised new boy, Marky had an outsider's perspective on band politics. 'Johnny never ran the show,' he now claims. 'He thought he did, but he didn't. His bark was bigger than his bite . . . Since Dee Dee was always high on something and Joey and Johnny didn't talk, I was asked a lot of time what I thought since a lot of the decision making was done on spite because of their animosity towards each other.'

Historically, the dynamism and excitement of rock 'n' roll has rarely transferred to the screen. For every *Rock Around the Clock*, or *Help!*, there have been plenty of flawed cash-ins and misguided vanity products. The assumption that musicians, as performers, can assimilate acting ability by osmosis has been proven false, chiefly by David Bowie and Sting. (Bowie can at least look back on one excellent performance, in *The Man Who Fell to Earth*, whereas Sting almost capsizes otherwise credible movies like *Lock, Stock and Two Smoking Barrels*.)

Given their reputation – and the image of punk rock in general – the Ramones made for unlikely matinee idols. However, in legendary exploitation maven Roger Corman, they would encounter a filmmaker who'd always been ready to take chances. Corman had directed such low-budget classics as *The Trip*, and a slew of Edgar Allan Poe adaptations with camp horror titan Vincent Price, before moving on to produce celebrated exploitation flicks like *Death Race 2000*.

Although Corman was originally planning to cash in on the disco craze, his collaborator and protégé Alan Arkush had convinced him to make a rock-orientated movie and identified frat-rockers Cheap Trick as suitable stars. The plan was jettisoned when it became obvious that a budget of $300,000 was too cheap for the Trick.

Director Arkush then homed in on the Ramones, who came to his attention via the unyielding support of Robert Christgau. Initially, the director was non-plussed by *Ramones*: 'Every song sounded alike, and I wasn't into the punk culture, so it didn't make sense.'

However, the album grew on him and he flew to New York to check out concerts at Hurrah's over 11-13 August. Impressed by the Ramones' visual image and unremitting aural assault, he approached the group to star in the film, which was to be entitled *Rock 'n' Roll High School*. Ever keen to reach new audiences, Fields and his charges readily agreed,

Punk *magazine's 1978 calendar was soon out-of-date due to Tommy's departure.*

leaving Arkush with the small matter of explaining to Corman who the Ramones actually were. He enlightened his mentor by showing him the *Mutant Monster Beach Party fumetti* from *Punk* magazine – featuring the Ramones, Andy Warhol, Debbie Harry, John Cale, David Johansen and others in a Corman-inspired romp.

The filming of *Rock 'n' Roll High School* began in early December at an abandoned former Catholic school in Watts, Los Angeles. The Ramones were relieved to be on the set in one piece, having recently endured a hail of missiles (including a pickaxe) thrown by punk-hating headbangers while supporting Black Sabbath in San Bernardino.

They had also been recording three new songs for the film soundtrack: 'Rock 'n' Roll High School', 'Come On Now' and 'I Want You Around'. (The soundtrack album also contained a live medley of Ramones tracks, plus the inevitable school-themed songs: Chuck Berry's 'School Days', Brownsville Station's 'Smokin' In The Boys Room', 'School's Out' by Alice Cooper.)

The premise of the film itself was simple fare: An evil, rock-hating high school principal, Miss Togar (played by Mary Woronov), is bent on keeping her students away from pernicious influences – particularly the Ramones. Keen to illustrate her point, she conducts experiments involving laboratory mice and loud rock music. Naturally, exposure to the Ramones causes the rodents to smoke pot and drop out.

Coincidentally, the band happens to playing in town, so the nefarious Miss Togar forbids all students to attend the show. This is a massive blow to the hopes of our heroine, Riff Randell (played by scream queen P. J. Soles), who just happens to be the band's number one fan.

Ha-ha-hilarious mayhem ensues, and the school blows up at the end. The Ramones don't have much in the way of lines to deliver, and spend much of their time on screen either miming to their songs or chomping pizza. As a pastiche of Fifties high school movies, the film is a pleasant enough piece of fluff. Conceived as a cult movie, this aim was inadvertently fulfilled by a limited distribution. (In the UK, it often appeared as part of a double bill with a low-grade slasher movie.) Despite this, it was a blast for Ramones fans to see da brudders on film – although why Concorde Pictures would choose to make a 1991 sequel, which the band wisely turned down, defies understanding.

Michael Jackson is taking six months to film *The Wiz*. I can't imagine us taking six months to do something like that. We're a rock group. We wanna play. We like to go out and do concerts. *Dee Dee Ramone*

The Ramones found hanging around all day waiting to shoot their scenes a huge drag, and left the set to play concerts whenever possible. Their devotion to gigging was more out of necessity than commitment, as their fee for the movie was a miserly $5,000.

Dee Dee and Marky spent most of their free time getting loaded, resulting in an overdose of Quaaludes, a bust and a trip to hospital for the bassist. Johnny was stoical about working on the film, viewing it as simply another 'job', while Joey saw it as a glorious opportunity for the group to raise its profile. While they were waiting for it to happen they returned to full-scale touring, seeing out the year on a double headliner in San Jose with contrived theatre-rock troupe the Tubes.

The Ramones remained convinced that huge global success was simply a question of adjusting their formula, and began planning their next album as they toiled across America in the early part of 1979. It had been nearly two years since they first caught the attention of Sixties production supremo Phil Spector. Meanwhile, the man responsible for the 'Wall of Sound', and the meteoric chart successes of the Ronettes, the Crystals and the Righteous Brothers, had been tracking the band's – and particularly Joey's – progress.

'Phil would call up,' Joey explained, 'and say, "What did you think of your last album?" I'd say, "Well, it's great." But then he'd say, "Why? Maybe next time we could all make a real rock 'n' roll record, a great record instead of just a good record?"'

Eventually, worn down by lack of commercial success and impressed by Spector's credentials, the band acquiesced. On 1 May, work commenced on their collaborative album, *End Of The Century*. Danny Fields and Seymour Stein were more than aware of Spector's reputation for eccentric behaviour. However, with the band coming to a creative and commercial impasse, it was felt they had little to lose. Obviously, as he'd been in virtual retirement for some years, there was plenty of publicity to be garnered from working with the producer. As Joey later pointed out, 'Phil quit loafing to produce us. It was two walls of sound that crash and sooner or later the sparks would come out, but working with him really was exciting.'

However, Johnny was less than keen, pegging Spector as 'another wacko from the Sixties. Phil'd be nice to me,' he continued, 'but so mean to everybody. He's a little man. He's got his wig on. He's got his lifts in his shoes. He's carrying his four guns. This guy's full of insecurities. I didn't want to work with him . . . [but] we were going to need help, because I already thought we were going to become big and I would be retired by my fifth album. And then I could see we were in trouble.'

Another negative aspect was that Tommy, an integral part of the band's extended family, was no longer required behind the mixing desk. 'The record companies always think there is the magic producer,' observed Tommy. 'The thing is, a lot of those guys – they've already done their magic albums. Besides, this is art. Sometimes it doesn't sell at first. Sometimes it takes a while for the world to catch on.'

Tommy's co-producer on the past two albums, Ed Stasium, was retained to help the band adjust to their new producer. 'Phil always wanted to produce the Ramones, ever since he saw them at the Whiskey years before,' Stasium recalls. 'And he was convinced that that record was going to be the biggest record ever made, bigger than *Hotel California* . . . I actually played guitar with the Ramones on all the tracking for that record. I also had to save the day a couple times because of Phil's eccentricities, to say the least.'

Spector's 'eccentricities' have been well documented

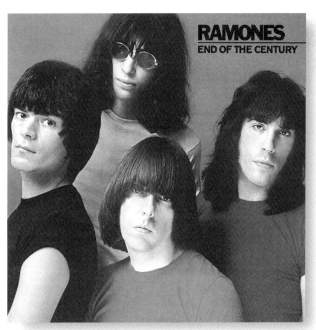

End Of The Century – *the Ramones vs. Phil Spector.*

over the years. In February 2003, they would land him at the centre of a full-blown murder investigation. As a fundamental rule, firearms, alcohol and paranoia make for a combustible mix – but these are three of the elements that define Phil Spector.

To exacerbate matters, relationships within the band were at a new low. Resentment against Johnny was at an all-time peak, and Marky's drinking, and Dee Dee's habit(s), hardly made for clear lines of communication.

'It was probably very rare that we were all talking,' recalls Johnny. 'For the first four albums, I think we were basically friends at heart. We got used to working like that. It got harder when records had to be made.'

In his autobiography, *Poison Heart*, Dee Dee gives his own perspective: 'The Ramones couldn't accept Marc, and he realised it. We stopped getting along and drinking together because of the tension. By then, the Ramones had a no-alcohol policy that I couldn't conform to and neither would Marc. I started fighting with Johnny Ramone because I felt the band were blaming me for all our failures. I was the most fucked up and the weakest one in the band and I was starting to hate their guts.'

You gotta be a punk and play punk rock. *Johnny Ramone*

Spector was fascinated by Joey's distinctive voice, and somewhat crestfallen to discover he was working with a *band* – as opposed to a vocalist and his backing musicians. 'It excited me because he loved my voice,' confessed Joey. 'He would say to me, "I'm going to make you the new Buddy Holly." As for the rest of the Ramones – they thought he was trying to steal me away.'

Spector invited the band to meet with him at his Beverly Hills mansion. Having given them a brief tour, he spirited Joey away for a 'private conference' – leaving Johnny, Dee Dee and Marky to stew in another part of the house.

'After about three hours I was getting restless,' recounted Dee Dee. 'I got up off the couch and tried to find Phil and Joey to see what was up. Phil must have thought I was an intruder. I really don't know what provoked him, but the next thing I knew Phil appeared at the top of the staircase, shouting and waving a pistol. Then he practically field-stripped the thing in two seconds flat.'

After everything cooled down, it was established that Joey would remain part of the band and that Dee Dee was not an assailant. When work got underway some days later, the difference between Spector's painstaking aural constructions and Johnny's one-take approach caused immediate tensions. As Stasium recalls, 'Phil made the band play constantly, do more takes than they had ever done in their lives.'

It ran totally contrary to Johnny's nature. During the recording of the title track, events came to a head. After a period spent on the opening chord, described by Joey as 'interminable', Johnny reached the end of his patience. As he motioned to leave the studio, Spector barked at him to return to his guitar duties. 'Phil says, "You're not going

Hey hey! We're the Ramones! Johnny, Joey, Dee Dee and Marky pose for Dutch TV.

anywhere,"' Johnny recalls. 'I said, "What are you going to do, shoot me?"' A meeting between the band, their management, Stasium and Spector was required to prevent work grinding to a halt. An understanding was reached. As Stasium later revealed, 'Phil agreed not to torture Johnny anymore.'

Although peace had broken out, Johnny was still less than enamoured with Spector's studio method. 'He wasn't a pleasant person,' Johnny confirms. 'He was nice to us, but he's just so horrible to everyone else around . . . It really worked when he got to a slow-er song like "Danny Says" – the production really worked tremendously. "Rock 'n' Roll Radio" is really good. For the harder stuff, it didn't work as well . . . And once they were going to bring in an orchestra to play on "Baby I Love You", I said, ". . . I ain't playing with no orchestra. That's not me."'

Dee Dee also found his creative input marginalised. 'I don't remember playing very much on it,' he admitted. 'I'm sure I didn't play on every track. I don't like that album. I didn't write anything good on it, unfortunately. That was my worst effort.'

Marky, on the other hand, bonded with Spector over booze. 'He knew that I liked wine,' Marky says. 'But he was drinking Manishewitz. I said, "Look, try the good Italian wines." He would come to my room at the Tropicana Hotel. Then we'd drive around in his Cadillac all night. With his bodyguards.'

This sat uneasily with Johnny, who was beginning to see how the producer was widening the rifts within the group. 'Mark and Joey were huge Phil Spector fans and what he was doing that was rotten, they didn't care. Dee Dee hated him. Dee Dee stayed a punk throughout.'

Given Spector's obsessive manner and exalted reputation, it's hardly surprising that *End Of The Century* turned out to be the Ramones' most expensive album – coming in at around $200,000. This was a horrifying amount of money for a band that was hardly a golden goose.

Despite having recorded five albums and played hundreds of gigs, Dee Dee was struggling to finance his smack habit on his $150-a-week allowance. Having discharged their recording duties in around three weeks, the band returned to the road while Spector whiled away the next five months neurotically mixing and remixing the album. 'When it was ready Phil wanted to mix it again,' Dee Dee complained.

Spector had also utilised a number of additional musicians to fill out the sound and cover Johnny and Dee Dee's sporadic absences. 'The guests had to save it,' Dee Dee confessed. 'They made an impression on the way things were recorded, and we're lucky we had them. I think I played my bass parts, but everybody tried to help make the record. Thank God Ed Stasium was there, and Jim Keltner, and the other tall guys [additional guitarists Dan and David Kessell].'

End Of The Century may well have been a traumatic studio experience, but the finished album is an exceptional *gestalt* of producer and band. The rich layering of Spector's textured multi-tracking and the incorporation of additional musicians may run contrary to the Ramones' minimalist ethos, but the album has a resonance and timbre few other producers could have matched.

Just as *Ramones* was indicative of the impact of the New York Dolls and the Stooges upon the band, *End Of The Century* thunderously evoked their earlier bubblegum-pop influences. This is particularly apparent in songs like 'Do You Remember Rock 'n' Roll Radio?', 'Rock 'n' Roll High School', and the cover of the Ronettes' 'Baby I Love You', where the production enhances and sweetens the Ramones sound. One of the outstanding tracks on the album is Joey's achingly tender account of life on the road, 'Danny Says' (after the band's manager, covered in 2002 by the Foo Fighters). Elsewhere, 'This Ain't Havana' and 'The Return Of Jackie And Judy' find the band returning to familiar themes with verve and humour.

A consistently upbeat album, *End Of The Century* contains none of the preoccupations with insanity that were prominent on *Road To Ruin*. The cover has a sunny glow, an innovation suggested by photographer Mick Rock. Joey and Dee Dee outvoted Johnny, and appeared without their leather jackets in primary coloured t-shirts (though Dee Dee snagged himself a suitably hoodlum-ish black number).

Further incongruity is provided by the inclusion of 'Chinese Rocks': an ode to the junkie lifestyle, rather out of place on an album packed with innocent exuberance. Originally written by Dee Dee in 1976, 'Chinese Rocks' had been rejected by the band for taking the concept of substance abuse a little too far for Johnny's liking. Junkie *par*

Joey hanging out in the Bowery, 1978.

Joey's vocal sensitivity caused Phil Spector to try and pry him away from the band.

excellence Johnny Thunders had no such qualms, and released his version of the song as a single. Some minor tampering with the lyrics was undertaken, and, when the record came out in May 1977, Thunders emerged with writing credits.

A minor storm-in-a-teaspoon ensued. 'Dee Dee wrote it,' confirmed Joey. 'In those days, Johnny didn't want songs about heroin. So Dee Dee got real frustrated and he took it over to Johnny Thunders of the Heartbreakers. That was his clique: Johnny Thunders and Richard Hell. The Heartbreakers copped the song and it became their anthem.'

Employing the same logic that Black Sabbath used when they insisted their early lyrics were a warning against Satanism, Dee Dee observed, 'I don't know if anybody's gonna listen, y'know, but it's a good idea to write an anti-drug song, to try and discourage them from using the stuff.'

End Of The Century was released in January 1980 to almost universally positive reviews. *Time Magazine*'s Jay Cocks described the album as, 'The kind of virtuoso feat one expects from Spector, but it is livelier and more intense than anything he's done since his work with John Lennon.' The magazine also named *End Of The Century* as one of the albums of the year.

In *Rolling Stone*, Kurt Loder claimed it was 'the most commercially credible album the Ramones have ever made, as well as Spector's finest and most mature effort in years.' The album proved to be the Ramones' biggest chart success, peaking at number 44 – not quite the level of success the band had been hoping for, although some consolation was found when 'Baby I Love You' crashed into the UK Top Ten.

Ironically, the single is almost a Joey solo effort. Depending on when he was asked, Dee Dee would tell differing stories as to his involvement, and Marky's drums were supplemented by Jim Keltner. But the combination of swirling strings, overblown arrangement and Joey's fragile voice was precisely what Spector had in mind. As writer and publicist B. P. Fallon explains, 'Down the line Phil gets to produce the Ramones and he takes this Joey voice, this perfect pop voice for today people and he melds it to "Baby I Love You", and God forgive me but it's as good as Ronnie Spector's immaculate vocal on the Phil Spector produced original by the Ronettes. But while Mrs. Spector had sang it with wet-lipped joy and celebration, in Joey's reading it was as if he was pleading his love. It was beautiful.'

The success of 'Baby I Love You' led to a bizarre *Top of the Pops* appearance. Union rules decreed that, as the song featured orchestral accompaniment, the band had to be filmed complete with a full orchestra. The sight of the Ramones backed by the BBC London Orchestra, dressed as if for a night at the Albert Hall, was a long way from Rockaway Beach.

Although 'Baby I Love You' ultimately failed to propel the Ramones to international stardom, the additional exposure brought Joey some new admirers. As his mother, Charlotte Lesher, revealed, 'He gets these propositions from 40-year-old women who want his fair body. I think he gets a charge out of that.'

Bad boys on the back seat. The Ramones on the endless highway.

We're A
Happy Family

We know a lot about life now, y'know, we're very experienced and very wise. *Dee Dee Ramone*

During the extended production period for *End Of The Century,* managers Danny Fields and Linda Stein were unceremoniously fired. It was announced in the new album's small print, with a new name credited under 'management': Gary Kurfirst.

When Fields and Stein's five-year contract with the Ramones had expired, the band opted to look elsewhere for a manager who could lead them to that elusive commercial utopia. 'The Ramones had great success playing live, but the effort of having [or at least aspiring to] an album in the Top Ten exhausted them, so they started looking for a new manager,' Stein admitted. 'I can't blame them for it, five years of activity playing all over the world, they were famous but their songs were never heard on the radio.'

In his mid-thirties, Kurfirst had extensive promotional and management experience with a clientele that had spanned from Free to Talking Heads. 'The other bands that they'd paved the way for were passing them by, so they had to rebuild to stay alive,' he said of the Ramones, keen to get them moving again.

The tantalising whiff of mass exposure that 'Baby I Love You' had hinted at only added to feelings of frustration in the brudderhood. 'Things should have changed four years ago – then I thought the whole music business would be "revolutionised",' observed a dispirited Johnny. 'I looked around and I thought that us and the Sex Pistols were the two best bands at what we were doin'. And it was, uh, naïve thinking that why shouldn't the two best bands be the two biggest bands. I realised soon after that the music business wanted to suppress the whole thing because they didn't understand it.'

Another issue facing the newly-installed Kurfirst was worsening personal relations within the group. Having experienced Johnny's rigid attitude to his drinking, Marky was well aware of the fraught atmosphere. 'Me and Dee Dee were the closest,' he acknowledged in 1999. 'Johnny and Dee Dee didn't really like each other. Dee Dee always complained that Johnny didn't contribute to the song writing, but he would get credit on the songs. That irked him, and the fact that Johnny took Joey's girlfriend away from him in 1981, which caused a lot of friction in the band. That festered until the band retired in '96. Johnny and Joey didn't talk to each other for eighteen years.'

Joey was heartbroken over this double betrayal, and upped his alcohol intake accordingly. Johnny and new partner Linda eventually married, while Joey would avoid further long-term relationships for fear of getting hurt. 'Johnny crossed the line with me concerning my girlfriend,' admitted Joey. 'If you want the band to blossom, get to its fullest, you don't cross that line. And I never felt any love for John anyways.'

But the fact that vocalist and guitarist were to spend nearly two decades locked in an environment of bitterness, rather than leaving or breaking up the group, is testament to the Ramones' collective doggedness. But it hardly made for camaraderie.

'Anytime Joey would want to relay a message to Johnny, he would have to go through me and vice versa. And they'd be standing three-four feet away from each other,' explained Marky.

Ramone and wife – Vera and Dee Dee hit the town.

Dee Dee was no stranger to domestic high drama either. Although the bassist had regularly claimed from the earliest interviews that he was married, in actuality he only tied the knot as recently as September 1978. 'When Dee Dee married Vera,' claimed Arturo Vega, 'I thought it was a good thing – anything that would help keep Dee Dee under control.' Despite his penchant for mayhem, the bassist was devoted to his wife and attempted to maintain a normal domestic arrangement.

To a few Americans it is given that they shall invent the perfect artefact for their time: Creole Sebastian Chaveau the marshmallow in 1868; ex-big band pianist Ray Kroc the McDonald's (as we know it) in 1954; New York's post-teens, John Cummings, Jeffrey Hyman, Douglas Colvin and Thomas Erdelyi, the Ramones in 1976. The best thing about achievements of this stature is that they endure and gather strength with the passage of time. *Cynthia Rose,* NME

The relationship with Vera certainly caused him a lot less aggravation and heartache than had his previous long-term girlfriend, Connie. As a couple, Dee Dee and Connie had plenty in common; a liking for junk, an appetite for chaos, and a background in hustling. Dee Dee later recounted his first impressions: 'One night, as I was leaving CBGB's at four in the morning, I walked outside and saw Connie sitting on the hood of a car, filing her nails . . . She was wearing a black evening dress and spiked, high-heel shoes, and she had a bottle of blackberry brandy in her purse. She looked like an ancient vampire countess who was definitely on a mission to capture my soul . . . She was a prostitute, I was a Ramone, and we were both junkies.'

Such a combination made for an uneasy relationship, and, as photographer Bob Gruen observed, she wasn't about to let him go easily: 'Dee Dee had been with Connie, and she was really on his case, being a real terror, and her psycho energy was driving him crazy.' Both parties were susceptible to bouts of chemically-induced paranoia, leading to fierce jealousies and bitter quarrels. 'She was just as crazy as I was,' admitted Dee Dee, 'we got kicked out of everywhere because of our violent arguments.' Ultimately, Dee Dee found the relationship too much of a liability and dumped Connie, penning 'Glad To See You Go' by way of a fond farewell. Both parties returned to their respective callings.

'After Dee Dee was with Vera, I started seeing Connie a lot on Third Avenue, working as a prostitute,' Vega described. Connie's patch was adjacent to Joey's apartment, causing Dee Dee to run into her on a number of occasions. He made well-intentioned attempts to help her out but they were unsuccessful. 'Prostitution is an addiction,' Dee Dee observed. 'I think hers had been a continuous lifestyle from day one.'

Vera, by contrast, was patient and understanding with Dee Dee, but less than enamoured of his old flame. 'Johnny Ramone told me that Connie had died,' Dee Dee explained. 'I couldn't mourn because I was with Vera. I couldn't show any emotion because Vera was jealous. The last time I saw Connie she was turning tricks. I used to go in the van and wait for them to pick up Joey in front of his apartment building and Connie was always working that area. She looked pretty bad. I don't know why anybody would love her, but I did.'

The band's disintegrating mental and physical state was aggravated by a world tour that took in Japan, Australia and New Zealand – in addition to their customary treks around North America and Europe. 'We kept playing, it was a way of life,' explained Dee Dee.

In addition to New York, Montreal, Berlin, Rome and London, the Ramones took care to play in less fashionable towns such as Canterbury and Lund, Sweden. 'You can't just go to a big city and play,' Marky offered. 'What about the kid who doesn't live in a big city? He's a human being too. He wants to see his favourite band.'

The Ramones actually took a month off in November 1980, before returning to the road and heading into the studio to cut some demos with Ed Stasium. The sessions, at the Daily Planet Studios in New York, would produce half a dozen songs that found their way onto the band's sixth studio offering, *Pleasant Dreams*. However, disagreements over production led to Stasium being ousted in favour of an outsider again.

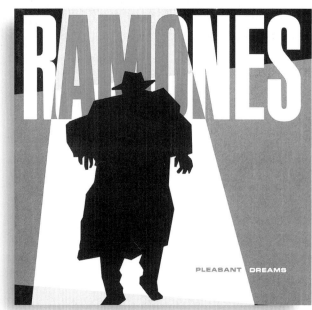

The strange cover of Pleasant Dreams *was the first Ramones sleeve not to depict the band.*

'We had Graham Gouldman as producer, and he was a very lightweight pop guy,' recalled Johnny. 'I knew I was in trouble immediately on the first day when he said, "Your amp is buzzing too much. Can you turn down your volume?" . . . He wasn't really right for the Ramones, that's all. We had no choice at that point in time. As far as producers, once you don't have the commercial success it's hard to maintain as much control over things as you'd like.'

Gouldman had been a member of 10cc, and had written hits for Herman's Hermits, the Hollies and the Yardbirds. Johnny was finding

Brand new Cadillac: the all-American brudders take to the road.

the sessions difficult, ostracised by Joey, irritated by Marky's drinking and Dee Dee's holistic approach to substance abuse.

The guitarist was thinking of throwing in the towel. 'Ideally I would've liked to have gotten really big and stopped after five years,' he admitted. 'And gone out somewhere around *End Of The Century*, where we would've been big enough where people were interested in me, and then I would've gotten into some aspect of film.' After the neurotic rollercoaster ride that was the Phil Spector experience, however, Dee Dee was pleasantly surprised by Gouldman's relaxed attitude, describing him as 'a gentleman'.

The album was released in July 1981 and climbed to number 58 on the *Billboard* chart. The band had generally felt that Gouldman's emphasis on harmony was a step too far into pure pop, only sounding off once it became apparent that *Pleasant Dreams* would not provide the desired chart breakthrough.

But the usual positive reviews followed, with *NME*'s Cynthia Rose particularly effusive: '*Pleasant Dreams* is that LP the Ramones have always dreamt of making . . . wholly realised songs, framed with non-stop pop expertise by producer Graham Gouldman (ex-10cc) and lovingly set in a running order, which not only accelerates but also, in doing so, accentuates Exactly What The Ramones Got That Nobody Else Has. What is that, you're asking? Well, for starters: stories, plots, a heritage, recognisable characters, tremendous language, colourful location work, overdrive, excitement, poetry, rhythm . . .'

In *Zigzag*, Marts Andrups cited the album as a step in the right direction: 'Joey's sickly vocals sound better than ever, and Marky is continually justifying his birthright in one of the only true pop groups left on this desolate planet. Now the Ramones are even dividing up their song writing credits (what can this signify, I wonder?).'

What it signified was the lack of unity. And that Joey and Dee Dee were demanding to be recognised as the main creative forces. 'Joey was doing a lot of extra work for the band,' explained Dee Dee. 'He probably felt that he was carrying the whole load and wanted credit for it.' Of the twelve songs on the album, seven were composed by Joey and five by Dee Dee.

I don't see Culture Club and Duran Duran being any role models for kids . . . they'll give you the incentive to go out and buy a blow-dryer or a synthesizer. *Joey Ramone*

Pleasant Dreams suffers in comparison with any of the band's earlier efforts, but is by no means to be found wanting. Joey's 'The KKK Took My Baby Away' is an anthemic stomper with a surf feel, the title referring both to Johnny's right-wing attitudes and his personal betrayal of the vocalist. On the whole, the album has a downbeat feel despite its pop tone. Joey's 'Don't Go', 'It's Not My Place (In The Nine To Five World)' and 'This Business Is Killing Me' are indicative of a troubled man, while '7-11' finds him in lovelorn mode.

The upbeat 'She's A Sensation' is a slice of classic Ramones pop, but was passed over as a single in favour of 'We Want The Airwaves' – a leaden appeal to radio programmers that was always likely to have the opposite effect. Dee Dee's input was inconsistent, although 'All's Quiet On The Eastern Front' was an enjoyably creepy midnight ramble, and 'Come On Now' provided the album with its customary Sixties homage.

In a further break with tradition, the cover of *Pleasant Dreams* had no picture of the band. Described by John Holmstrom as 'one of the ugliest record covers of all time', it featured the silhouetted figure of a stalker under a yellow spotlight – possibly alluding to Dee Dee's 'All's Quiet On The Eastern Front', it was not what the Ramones faithful had come to expect.

As Graham Gouldman moved on to his next project – an album with diminutive Brit troubadour Gilbert O'Sullivan – the Ramones returned, inevitably, to the road. Unusually, they confined their tour to the USA. In Britain, the fury of punk had given way to a series of media-led Sixties revivals (power pop, mod, ska) and the Thatcherite drag of new romanticism.

Joey was having none of it: 'We didn't go Blondie's route and go disco and we're not gonna become a ska band and play reggae.' The band had also tired of being caricatured as 'dumb' by British journalists such as the reliably precious Tony Parsons, who used a January '78 *NME* article as a showcase for his anti-American xenophobia of the time. Dee Dee had been a particular target.

'Just by reading his lyrics how could you think he was dumb?' asked Joey. 'I think he's real articulate. There were things that came out in the press that I wasn't too thrilled about. In fact, at one time I didn't wanna do another interview with the British press . . . it was sick. They'd start ripping apart your household, your mother. It was crazy.'

An obviously hurt Dee Dee took a philosophical view. 'I don't know why they did that to me but . . . I don't think I'm dumb. I think I'm a very sensitive, deep thinking person. I have a lot of knowledge about life. I've led a very deep and experienced life and I've a lot of knowledge that an older man probably wouldn't have.'

Still, it was becoming apparent that the band were treading water. They were rooted in a seemingly endless cycle of touring and recording without any real increase in success or status. Sire were promoting their records less, there was little encouragement for the band to tour abroad, and 'We Want The Airwaves' was to be the last Ramones single in the US for five years.

This entropy was in evidence when they entered New York's Kingdom Sound studio to begin work on their next album, *Subterranean Jungle*. The studio was located in Long Island, and guaranteed a couple of additional hours' van time each day. The quarrelsome quartet seemed in no shape to be recording an album, with Joey's weakening voice adding to the general malaise.

They were unhappy with the studio, had little new material written, and were upset at having producers Richie Cordell and Glen Kolotkin thrust upon them. The original choice, Kenny Laguna, was managing former Runaway Joan Jett and was too busy to take the assignment. Laguna suggested Cordell, who had co-produced Jett's recent hit reworking of 'I Love Rock 'n' Roll'. Kolotkin, in partnership with Cordell, came along with the package.

Disappointed with a production team who lacked the *cachet* to broaden their audience, yet aspired to further softening the Ramones sound, the group initially gave the duo a rough ride. 'I was so upset after fifteen minutes that I tried to leave and walked into a closet,' recalled Cordell.

Further problems were caused by Marky, who was in the grip of a serious alcohol addiction and displayed increasingly bizarre behaviour on the road. 'Marky gave Monte [Melnick] the nickname "Lambie",' recounted Dee Dee. 'Marky would work himself up into a frenzy in the van, making lamb noises until Monte would flip. Then "the Lamb" would threaten to drive us off the road and he would step on the gas. He would get the wild sheep-eyed look and a beet-red face and start shouting, "We're all going to perish now, you fucking creeps . . . because you wouldn't shut up. You're the lamb, Marc! You! You! You!"'

More significantly, the drinking had caused Marky to break the band's cardinal rule – he had missed a show, and let the fans down. As he recalls, 'We were in Cleveland, I stayed up all night and the next morning I was completely far out. That evening we had to play at Virginia Beach but I started drinking and got drunk. I had to go to the air-port, but I lost the plane and although I wanted to rent a plane they wouldn't let me go on because I was too drunk.'

The show was later re-scheduled, but, so far as Johnny was concerned, Marky had to go. '*Subterranean Jungle* would have been basically a pleasant experience,' he claims, 'but we were having trouble with Marky. He was replaced when the sessions ended . . . We were starting to get back on track. Me and Dee Dee were at least talking at that point.'

Given the hostile relations between the band, it's surprising that *Subterranean Jungle* happened at all. Kurt Loder in *Rolling Stone* appraised it as 'another masterful blast of the sort that will one day earn the Ramones a special place in the rock pantheon,' but it real-ly only stands up as a solid, if over-produced, piece of early 1980s American rock. The inclusion of three cover versions ('Little Bit O' Soul', 'I Need Your Love' and 'Time Has Come Today'), while proficiently executed, indicated a paucity of new songs.

Although Joey contributed the excellent 'Every Time I Eat Vegetables It Makes Me Think Of You', Dee Dee carried the bulk of the album's writing. A brief return to early form, 'Psycho Therapy' was co-written with Johnny and is the pick of the bassist's six tracks, while the autobiographical 'Outsider' and the anthemic rock of 'Highest Trails Above' and 'In The Park' keep the tempo moving. Additional gui-tar was provided by former Heartbreaker Walter Lure, with another former Thunders man, Billy Rodgers, occupying Marky's vacant stool for 'Time Has Come Today'.

Marky's final dismissal came courtesy of some text-book junkie hypocrisy from Dee Dee, who discovered the drummer's vodka stash. 'I hid it in the garbage, Dee Dee

The cover of Subterranean Jungle *hinted at Marky's imminent departure from the band.*

found it and ratted on me,' accused Marky. 'After that I got a call – "We don't want you in the band anymore."'

The marginalisation of Marky was completed by relegation to an inset on the album sleeve. Although an improvement on *Pleasant Dreams*, the cover of *Subterranean Jungle* is a sloppy affair. Depicting the band on a heavily-graffitied subway train, Marky appears to be peering out of a window, his head nearly twice as big as Johnny's. Dee Dee's t-shirt has been airbrushed, giving him a v-neck vest whiter than anything he ever wore.

Joey, seen crouching like a mantis at the back of the shot, was surprisingly upbeat about the album: 'With *Subterranean Jungle* we were us again. After *End Of The Century* we couldn't stand the sight of each other anymore.'

The loyalty of the Ramones fan base ensured that *Subterranean Jungle* crept into the *Billboard* chart at number 82, in February 1983. In the press, Ramoniac Cynthia Rose's enthusiasm was undiminished: 'This band is staring into the absolute face of the void with more than confidence – this is triumphant music. Why is this possible? Essentially because the Ramones remain humble at heart and still simply love what they do.'

In the six years since the punk explosion of 1977, the bands of that era had diversified or split. While the Clash, Blondie and Talking Heads were enjoying chart success by moving away from their original sounds, the Ramones were discovering that this wasn't going to work for them. *Subterranean Jungle* would be the last Ramones album which held any realistic hope of commercial success.

We're writing as mature adults. *Dee Dee Ramone*

More positively, a new generation of punk bands had emerged on both sides of the Atlantic. In Los Angeles and San Francisco, the hardcore scene had developed around a multitude of bands like the Dead Kennedys, the Circle Jerks, the Germs and Black Flag. In Britain, anarcho-punk pioneers like Crass and Discharge dominated the independent charts alongside the skinhead-punk of the Cockney Rejects and the Exploited.

Faster, more aggressive and less diverse than the original punk rockers, the new bands owed much to the Ramones and acted as an introduction for younger punks who missed the first wave. 'We're very popular with the hardcore movement,' enthused Dee Dee. 'They didn't like us in the beginning, but now they like us a lot and they all come and see us. The concerts are gettin' really crazy, almost too crazy.'

Joey was equally excited. 'I think it's great, it's an outlet of expression and it's very real and very honest. We just did a two-month tour in America and it was as wild as England used to be in the Seventies. We're even getting heavy metal fans who are disgusted with all the pop heavy metal bands and are looking for some real gut energy. They're, like, getting into Motorhead and us.'

Richie Reinhardt, aka Richie Beau, added to his list of aliases via induction into the Ramones in early 1983. Marky had graciously fulfilled his live commitments, playing his final gig in Long Island on 27 November. The group were now afforded a three-month

Anudda brudda – Richie (left) became the Ramones' third drummer in 1983.

period to recruit and rehearse their new drummer before the re-commencement of hostilities on 13 February.

Richie had been recruited from the new wave-dance act Velveteen, and had previously played in a number of minor New York bands. Any optimism generated by the line-up's return to full strength was tempered by the new contract offered by Sire/Warner. With little in the way of alternative offers, the Ramones signed a new three-album deal that made no provision for singles – tantamount to heresy for Joey who, despite all evidence to the contrary, still believed the band had hit-single potential. 'It's like somebody cutting your tongue out,' he protested. By way of consolation, the band received greater control over the selection of producers and were offered the chance to make promotional videos for future releases.

With Richie bedding in seamlessly, the Ramones' endless roadshow spent a solid five months travelling around the USA. It came to an abrupt, unpleasant halt on 15 August

1983 on their home turf of Queens, when Johnny became embroiled in a dispute with another punk musician, Seth Macklin, over his girlfriend of the time. The guitarist was seriously injured in a four a.m. brawl, when Macklin karate-chopped him to the ground before repeatedly kicking him in the head. Johnny suffered concussion and a fractured skull that required surgery.

He later claimed to recall little of the attack: 'I never saw what happened or what led up to it. The kid got arrested and went to jail.' Although the incident took the band off of the road until December, it brought the group closer together than for some time. The break also allowed Dee Dee and Joey the opportunity to experience the developing hardcore scene, and by the time the band returned to the studio, in July 1984, the pre-vailing vibe was far more positive than it had been for *Subterranean Jungle*.

Hardcore is a big thing here now; Dee Dee's really into that. There's a lotta new spots you can go to hear it, it's a real alternative. *Joey Ramone*

The Ramones provided much of the sonic inspiration for the hardcore movement, and, by way of return, received validation for their primitivism. When the band went to see the new groups, they realised there was nothing wrong in returning to their early simplicity of execution.

The new album, entitled *Too Tough To Die* after Johnny's recent trauma, was a return to fundamentals. The first step was to bring back Tommy Erdelyi and Ed Stasium to produce. As Johnny admitted, 'We always felt more comfortable with Tommy and Ed Stasium. Tommy always knew what we should sound like, and I think we always sounded best on the albums he worked on.'

However, Gary Kurfirst still had ideas about scoring a hit, and tendered the notion of Dave Stewart, of the Eurythmics, handling produc-tion. After some debate, it was

Too Tough To Die – *the atmospheric cover was the result of a misfiring flashgun.*

agreed that Stewart could produce one track for release as a single outside of the US, with Tommy and Ed handling the remainder of the album.

The single, 'Howling At The Moon (Sha-La-La)', was prettied up with some additional keyboards but made no impact on the UK chart. Despite its saccharine sound, it was indicative of the band's new social awareness. 'That was about Reagan, and how, like, he's made everything convenient for the rich now, and how the poor are really suffering in America,' explained Dee Dee. 'It was about how, like, a rich man can commit any crime he wants and get free with a real expensive lawyer and bribe the judge, but if a black kid in the ghetto gets busted with one joint they throw him in jail. It's like, what's going on here?'

As with its predecessor, the lion's share of writing on *Too Tough To Die* was by Dee Dee. 'We wanted to make a real Ramones record and recapture us,' explained the bassist. 'America is a pretty bleak place, there's no hope really. When we started out writing about politics and stuff all of a sudden it was, "Hey, the Ramones preaching left-wing propaganda." But that's how we felt. We wanted to show we had feelings. We've gotten serious with this album.'

We finally were out of the tunnel. In 1983/84 we touched the bottom and I was thinking of quitting or of recording a solo album. *Joey Ramone*

The hardcore influence is apparent on 'Wart Hog' and 'Endless Vacation', both written by Dee Dee and Johnny. Dee Dee delivers the vocal on both tracks, the frantic thrash-punk pace of the songs entirely unsuitable for Joey's voice. (An early demo of 'Endless Vacation' features Dee Dee hilariously reverting to type, Dr. Strangelove-style, bellowing 'Deutschland, Deutschland' as the track winds down.)

Dee Dee's newfound social conscience is also given an airing on 'Danger Zone', 'I'm Not Afraid Of Life' and 'Planet Earth 1988'. Joey, assisted by long-time Ramones associate and session-man Daniel Rey, returned to form with the sensitive and chart-worthy 'Daytime Dilemma (Dangers Of Love)'.

The title track of *TTTD* provides the album with one of its twin highlights, evoking the band's Stooges influence in thunderous manner. 'Chasing The Night', a collaboration between Joey, Dee Dee and Busta Jones, former bassist for Albert King, Sharks and Talking Heads, is soaring Ramones-pop of the highest order.

Johnny also increased his creative input, co-credited on five songs including the band's first instrumental, 'Durango 95'. Even Richie chips in with the slightly nondescript 'Humankind'. If there is one criticism of the album, it's a minor one – the Ramones' new political agenda was to the detriment of both their humorous content and their group charm. Overall though, it appeared da brudderhood was back on track.

'Bonzo Goes To Bitburg' demonstrated Joey's social conscience, much to Johnny's irritation.

There was little soul-searching when *Too Tough To Die* slumped at a peak of number 171 in the US chart. The album had done better business abroad, but so far as Joey was concerned chart placings were no longer an issue.

'These lyrics represent us whereas most bands just don't care anymore,' he claimed. 'There aren't that many that you can really respect . . . like Alice Cooper. When I first got into him in '72 I thought, "This guy is really sick!" Then I found out he was straight and I was real disgusted and upset. I thought the guy was a real sick necrophiliac and that was great. Ha! Ha! There really aren't many people you can really believe in . . .'

Despite still harbouring bitterness toward Johnny, Joey had come to view the Ramones as an extended family. He was delighted to welcome back Tommy and Ed and enthusiastic about their contributions: 'It has a real powerful sound – something we lost a little on the last two albums. I love those albums, but this one sorta restates a Ramones vision. And it's because the production is really there at last. I think the vocals are the best I've ever done too.'

However, Johnny was less than comfortable as part of a politicised Ramones. As a staunch Republican, he was aghast at this apparent tide of liberalism. 'I think punk should be right wing,' asserted the guitarist. 'The left wing is trying to destroy America by giving handouts to everyone and making everyone dependent on them . . . They don't care about anyone. If they can get illegal aliens to become able to vote by voter registration, they will. They're illegal aliens! They don't even belong in the country, let alone voting.'

Irrespective of Johnny's taxi-cab philosophising, the Ramones returned to the road in a near-harmonious state. 'Everybody's doing well,' gushed Joey. 'John's still a reclusive fellow, though. He likes to pop into the 7-11 after a gig, grab his milk and cookies and disappear. Richie likes to party and hang out a little more. He's a golfer. Every time we pass a golf course, it's like, "Oh there's a nice one!" . . . Richie's making it fun to be in the Ramones again.'

Life on the road was also made more bearable by travelling in comfort. 'A nice bus. Not what Billy Idol could travel in,' described Joey, 'but it's OK. It's got a video, it's got

enough room so we do not murder each other or anything. Everything's OK, everything's actually pretty good.'

The New Year heralded a new UK contract for the band, who signed with the independent label Beggar's Banquet – responsible for Gary Numan and Ramones-influenced
punks the Lurkers. This new association saw the band return to Britain for the first time
since 1981, for four nights at the Lyceum in London's West End.

Sadly, Joey found it disappointing in comparison with the triumphant scenes of nine
years earlier. 'All along, reading fan mail that we got from abroad, like France and England
and all over, the kids were saying, "Come over here and show us how to rock again." I feel
like the country's sleeping, there's really nothing going on. I remember years back when it
was really exciting, when it was explosive here, and now it's very conservative and dull.'

The Ramones' first single for their new label, 'Bonzo Goes To Bitburg', lampooned
President Ronald Reagan's decision to lay a wreath at a German cemetery where Nazi
stormtroopers were buried. Unsurprisingly, it failed to delight Johnny – who insisted on a
title change to 'My Brain Is Hanging Upside Down' when the song resurfaced as an album
track, and refused to play it live. Politically, the guitarist was sticking to his NRA-approved
guns. 'I thought Ronald Reagan was the best President of our lifetime,' he insists.

**We are sorta shy of talking about drugs, we don't wanna
remember them any more, and we're just happy we're still
alive, that none of us died or anything. I mean, I'm happier
now, I just have a Coke when we go to the bar.** *Dee Dee Ramone*

The band returned to almost full-time touring for the remainder of 1985, revisiting
Ireland, Denmark, Germany and Belgium and supporting U2 at the UK's Milton
Keynes Bowl. The upbeat mood of the previous few months endured, and the group
returned to the studio in December to begin work on *Animal Boy*. Given the positive
vibe of *Too Tough*, Tommy and Ed were surprised to find themselves supplanted as producers by Jean Beauvoir, the former member of shock rockers the Plasmatics who produced the 'Bonzo Goes To Bitburg' single.

In fact, the hardcore punk scene showed little sign of enduring, which led to the
abandonment of *TTTD*'s reductive approach. It brought a renewed sense of uncertain-
ty in the Ramones' direction, and they reacted by reverting to the bad old ways. Joey hit
the bottle and his songwriting dried up, his attitude exposed by the titles of his contributions, 'Mental Hell' and 'Hair Of The Dog'.

'It seemed as soon as I started to consider quitting drinking,' said Dee Dee, 'he started up. We'd have to go pick him up at a bar called Paul's on Tenth Street and drag him
to the recording studio.'

Dee Dee contributed to the group's fragmentation by spending most of a promotional tour of England hiding in his hotel room. Old hostilities resurfaced, with the bassist accusing Johnny of blocking his and Joey's creative ideas. The resultant album was an inconsistent mix of songs rendered bland by Beauvoir's standardised production. Most of the songs were composed by Dee Dee, often with assistance from Daniel Rey, with the highlight, 'Something To Believe In', showcasing Joey's ravaged-yet-heart-rending delivery. The album's only soaring pop clas-

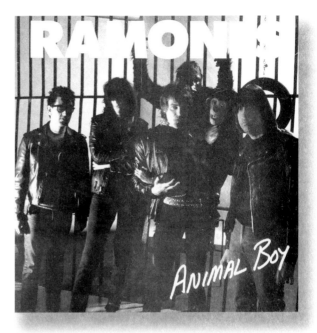

Animal Boy – Lacked the consistency that made the Ramones great.

sic, 'Something' became the Ramones first US single since 1981. In its promotional video, the band poked fun at the mid-Eighties slew of charity records by featuring a spokesman espousing 'Ramones Aid'. It was highly apt. Having just delivered their first truly lousy album, it was clear they were in need of some kind of help.

Ironically, *Animal Boy* managed a marginally higher chart placing than the far superior *Too Tough* – sliding in at number 147 on the *Billboard* chart in May 1986. In the UK, the album impacted on the lower reaches of the Top 40 thanks to enthusiastic marketing by Beggars Banquet.

While reviews remained generally favourable, longtime Ramones fan and critic Robert Christgau said the album was lacking 'the consistency that has made them great'. The Ramones were in decline, and it seemed there was little they could do to stop the rot.

From Joey's perspective the foursome had little option other than to remain themselves. 'It's been a hard road, it's never been easy. We never got any breaks. Seems like everybody else got the breaks, all the people that came later. We never fitted in any category, there was no niche for us. We are us. We are genuine, and we're not gonna fuckin' become pretty boys so we can fit in a niche and be played on MTV like Billy Idol.'

The group were retained by Sire/Warner, but only as a moderately successful live act who didn't sell enough product to target anyone other than a niche market of loyalists and retro-punks. With new budgetary restrictions, the Ramones' eleventh studio album in ten years would be produced as cheaply as possible.

Halfway To Sanity *was to be Richie's last album with the band.*

When work began on *Halfway To Sanity* in the spring of 1987, Daniel Rey was installed to produce. 'Instead of spending $20,000 for a famous producer, they thought about me,' Rey explained. 'That's the way Johnny is, attentive to cost and to fans' expectations.'

If those expectations were raised by the prospect of having an insider at the helm, they were to be dashed by the result. *Halfway To Sanity* had less to offer than the mediocre *Animal Boy*. Hampered by the Ramones' lack of direction and limited financial resources, Rey struggled to impart his natural enthusiasm for the band. But songs like 'I Wanna Live', 'Go Lil' Camaro Go' and 'Bop 'Til You Drop' are Ramones-by-numbers, imprinted with the hallmark of a band contractually obligated to make Just Another Album.

As the youngest Ramone, Richie had not yet had his aspirations knocked out of him. As a non-original member, however, he had no say in the band's decision-making and was treated as little more than a hired hand by Johnny. Still, the drummer had adapted well to the endless touring and contributed two new songs, 'I'm Not Jesus' and 'I Know Better Now'.

During the album's production, however, Richie became dissatisfied with the low budget and general gloom that pervaded at the sessions. Having recently married, Richie – egged on by his new wife – decided to approach Gary Kurfirst directly to secure a raise. No agreement was reached between drummer and management, so Richie threatened to leave the band mid-tour.

'He said he would do the New York shows for $500 a night,' Joey explained. 'I'm sure he felt he had us by the balls – our album was coming out and there was a lot of press coming.' But the Ramones refused to bow to their drummer's demands, and the following three nights' concerts were cancelled.

Keen to fulfil their tour obligations, the band immediately enlisted the former Blondie drummer Clem Burke. Despite his experience and skill, Burke (who settled on the name Elvis Ramone) found that matching the Ramones' breathless live pace was more important than technique.

'People think that anybody can play drums with the Ramones,' Monte Melnick explained. 'When Clem joined the band he asked Johnny how many beats he should play, the answer was: fast and faster. After two weeks he was out of the group.'

Burke managed only two concerts with the band. Describing the gigs as 'a disaster', Johnny recalled, 'He did his best but he didn't have the right style. He was too soft and didn't play the way we needed.'

With a string of US and European shows lined up, the band needed a drummer who could fit in instantly. There was no question of Clem continuing, and Richie, who'd departed to become a golf caddy, was *persona non grata*. The only realistic candidate was Marc Bell, who'd been through detox and formed his own band, M-80.

'We fixed a rehearsal with Marky to see how he was doing,' explained Johnny, 'after one song it was exactly as the Ramones should be. I called Joey and told him Marky was fantastic. Less than one week later Marky was back with us. We didn't have to cancel any gigs.'

On 4 September 1987, Marky Ramone played his first gig with the band for almost four years. Re-admitted to the dysfunctional brudderhood, the prodigal beat-keeper was delighted. 'I knew I had a job to do,' he claimed, 'to make people happy. All I ever wanted was to see smiles on the kids' faces.'

Dee Dee and Darryl McDaniel (Run DMC): the kings of rock and rap cross-fertilise in 1989.

Endless Vacation

We don't want to be remembered as a band that sucked at the end. *Marky Ramone*

Marky's return to the fold ensured the Ramones could embark on a series of tours for the next eighteen months. They recorded no new material during 1988, although Sire released a compilation double album, *Ramones Mania*, which provided the band with their first gold disc. 'I Wanna Be Sedated' was also re-released as a single, backed by a cheesy Ramones-on-45 medley.

The three original band members were scarcely on speaking terms, however. Joey and Dee Dee had broken ranks to make individual solo recordings – Dee Dee with an absurd rap single, 'Funky Man (Rock Hotel)', a wholehearted if inept effort to embrace hip-hop. Belatedly leaping on a bandwagon that the Clash and Blondie alighted on in the early Eighties, Dee Dee adopted the surname King – an indication of his growing alienation from the Ramones.

He was assisted in his folly by Daniel Rey. 'Dee Dee had been in the hospital for two weeks to detoxicate himself,' describes Rey. 'When he got out he was Dee Dee King the rapper and I helped him write part of the album but I didn't feel at ease: he was one of the Ramones and he couldn't be playing that stuff.'

But it wasn't the last the band would hear of their bassist's new fixation. He harboured an increasingly rebellious attitude towards the Ramones 'uniform', still insisted on by Johnny. 'I was getting sick of playing in a revival act,' Dee Dee explained. 'It made me feel like a phoney standing there in a leather jacket and torn jeans – like I used to dress when I thought I was a worthless piece of shit.'

Whereas Joey adopted leather trousers and gloves, Dee Dee cropped his hair and attempted to grow a beard. This determination to define his own style – and to irritate the hell out of Johnny – reached absurd proportions when he reported for promotional duties dressed like a precursor of Ali G. 'When I showed up for the video shoot for the Ramones' "I Wanna Live" in a maroon jumpsuit, gold chains and a Kangol that I'd bought at Doctor Jay's in Flushing, the rest of the band hit the ceiling,' confirmed Dee Dee. 'If they had had it with me at this point then fine, I'd sure had it with them.'

At least Joey's side-project was less crazy – a festive single entitled 'Merry Christmas (I Don't Want To Fight Tonight)'. Produced by Jean Beauvoir and Daniel Rey, the record was a rich exemplar of the vocalist's fascination with the Ronettes/Shangri-La's sound. It featured Marky on drums, and was later incorporated into the Ramones' set (unlike Dee Dee's rapping). 'I always felt it cool that the Ramones should have a Christmas song because Slade had that,' asserted Joey.

But the Ramones saw in 1989 amidst an atmosphere of rancour and substance abuse. The vocalist had developed a taste for cocaine, which, along with his heavy drinking, made touring an even greater physical burden. Dee Dee had been seeking psychiatric help for his various addictions, and had found himself on the mental ward on a number of occasions.

As Joey revealed, 'He went to the psychoanalyst every day, but then he quit his recovery program, he thought that everyone else was crazy and he didn't listen to anyone because he thought that they were enemies trying to harm him.'

Dee Dee was prescribed sedatives, which calmed him down but did little for his confused mental state. 'When he was really medicated, he was on a lot of mind-altering drugs that the doctors prescribed, he was really kind of a walking zombie,' explained Rey. 'Which was a trade off. Everyone – his wife, Monte, and the doctors seemed to want him to take them because it made him easier to control.'

Dee Dee's detachment from reality become ever more apparent when he released an entire album of rap-orientated material. *Standing In The Spotlight* was released in March 1989, and widely derided by all who heard it. 'As my alter ego, King is able to do a lot of things I've always wanted,' trumpeted Dee Dee.

Along with the newly crowned 'King of Rap', the rest of the band had spent much of the same month in the studio completing *Brain Drain*, an album that was to be their last for Sire. The album was produced by Bill Laswell, a rising producer who'd previously worked with Iggy Pop and Motorhead. Although by no means a clas-

Brain Drain *marked the end of the band's relationship with Sire and the last time Dee Dee would record as a Ramone.*

sic Ramones offering, *Brain Drain* provided an unexpected improvement on
Animal Boy and *Halfway to Sanity*.

As if to belie his dizzying descent into
addiction, Joey's contributions comprise
the disc's finest moments. In addition to
'Merry Christmas', the best is the engaging, Stephen King-inspired 'Pet
Sematary'. Sire would select the song as
their final Ramones single. Although it
merely skirted the charts, it demonstrated
the band could still produce songs that
stuck in the mind.

Despite his crumbling grip on reality,
Dee Dee weighed in with half a dozen
songs – all of which were co-written. The

Like **Road To Ruin,** *1989's* **Brain Drain** *highlighted the Ramones' gentler side.*

album received positive press and reached a higher chart position (number 122) than
anything since *Subterranean Jungle*. As ever, the Ramones went on tour to promote the
record – during which period they commemorated fifteen years together. So far as Dee
Dee was concerned, it was quite long enough.

In July, with the US tour over, he handed in his notice to Gary Kurfirst. With his
usual lack of sentimentality, Johnny scheduled auditions the next day. 'When Dee Dee
left,' he said later, 'I had people telling me, "You gotta stop now." That's ridiculous. I
can't accept defeat like that.'

For people afflicted by psychological problems, it's considered wise to avoid unpleasant, stressful or discomforting situations. Given the way the Ramones operated, it's surprising that Dee Dee remained in the band for so long.

'There was nobody who could write like him and he was one of the founders of punk
rock,' Marky later acclaimed. 'He couldn't take the bickering between Joey and Johnny,
so he left.' As Marky understood, a revolving door policy for drummers was one thing,
but losing one of the cornerstones of the band would have a more significant impact.

'I couldn't take it anymore, I was exasperated,' Dee Dee pleaded. 'The last studio
album was hell. There was a lot of grief. Joey was drinking a lot and very argumentative.
Johnny was a pain in the ass and always in a bad mood.'

'Dee Dee decided he wanted to go off and become a rap star,' mocked Joey – but he
later paid him fulsome tribute. 'I think about Dee Dee's contributions – I was listening
to *Too Tough To Die* the other day and I remember thinking when we recorded the
album how I thought his song "Planet Earth 1988" had such great lyrics. They were perfect – he's really got the knack. He's very fluent in his thinking and his execution. I think
Dee Dee respects me as a songwriter, and I respect him.'

'I didn't leave the Ramones to pursue a rap career,' countered Dee Dee. 'I had
become seriously ill. I was throwing up constantly, it was anorexia and bulimia. I was

sober, but had been taking anti-depressants, which made me fat. Nobody believed I was ill. Everybody was really cruel. I would throw up and they would all pretend to be concerned. It was so humiliating. Being in the van and listening to endless baseball games on the radio was driving me crazy.'

'Dee Dee left his wife Vera a month earlier and this could have been one of the reasons, a period of real mental instability,' opined Johnny, 'but I never thought he would quit. Do you think he did [it] for his solo career? It doesn't seem like he had a lot of benefits from it, or am I wrong?'

Ex-wife Vera offered her own perspective. 'It's been a lot of things combined, he quit drinking and using drugs five years ago, but was always on tour with the Ramones or writing and recording songs. He wrote every song more to satisfy Johnny than himself, he stayed sober more for me and the others for himself.'

Irrespective of his personal and pharmaceutical problems, the loss of Dee Dee posed a real threat to the Ramones. As even Johnny had to admit, 'a lot of the best stuff on those last records was written by Dee Dee.'

We could never be phoneys. The only thing we have to maintain is our dignity. In the future I'd like to write for other people and stuff but I don't want to put pressure on myself. I've already done everything now and I have to live the rest of my years as easy as I can. I hope I never have to get a job! *Dee Dee Ramone*

But Johnny wasn't quitting on anyone's terms but his own. Having accepted that the group were not going to achieve superstar status, the guitarist envisioned 'the job' lasting twenty years – with record and songwriting royalties as his pension. It was simply a question of seeing who turned up for the auditions, and carrying on as usual.

The first aspirant new Ramone was Christopher Joseph Ward, a 23-year-old mohawked punk, whose limited musical experience was as a guitarist. He was also technically absent without leave from the US Marines.

'Hi, I'm C.J.,' he introduced himself, 'I play the bass and I have three idols: Paul Simonon of the Clash, Sid Vicious and, obviously, Dee Dee. I'm ready!' C.J.'s enthusiasm made an immediate impact on Johnny, who was also taken with the youngster's military background. He was completely unlike Dee Dee, with no physical or stylistic resemblance, and was neither a junkie nor an alcoholic.

At the end of three days of auditions, Johnny's enthusiasm hadn't waned. 'I knew immediately,' he insisted. 'Marky and our road manager kept saying, "Nah. He's not good. He's young. He's inexperienced. He's got a mohawk. He plays with his fingers [as

C.J. (second from right) added youthful impetus to the road-weary Ramones.

opposed to using a plectrum, as Dee Dee did].' That didn't matter. All that mattered was the image.'

The guitarist pressed his arguments with typical doggedness, and C.J. became a Ramone. The next step was to get him out of the Marines. 'I was actually waiting on a discharge, so it wasn't like I deserted,' explained C.J. 'They [the Marine Corps] kept trying to send me out to Japan and I knew once I got there, it would be awfully hard to get a discharge, so I said fuck it . . . They arrested me and threw me in the brig. So, the first night I'm in jail I get a phone call from Johnny saying for me to do my time, and when I get out I've got a job.'

Once C.J.'s discharge was secured, Johnny set about putting the bassist through basic training. 'We had a mirror in front of us in the rehearsal room. I'd say, "C.J., face there. Don't look at Marc. Look in the mirror. When you see me go forward, you go forward. Get your bass down below your waist. Get your legs spread apart. Look forward, play forward." I always hated it, when bands did that other stuff – played to the amplifier, played to the drummer. We didn't play to each other.'

C.J. may have felt like he was back in boot camp, but he also looked the part. 'In the real early photographs you see of me and in the video [*Lifestyles of the Ramones*, a compilation of live footage, promo videos and interviews],' he observed, 'I've got a bandana around my head because they just shaved it from the brig. I was literally just a week out of jail.'

If C.J. had been hoping for a low-key live debut, he was to be disappointed. The rookie bassist made his entrance at an annual muscular dystrophy telethon, fronted by Jerry Lewis. 'C.J. was terrible,' recounted Johnny. 'There was so much excitement he forgot all the rehearsals. He moved too much, although I told him to do it only when he felt at ease. And he cut his finger playing "Blitzkrieg Bop" with too much enthusiasm.'

C.J. remembers the gig with characteristic ebullience: 'It was my baptism of fire. I went on stage completely out of my mind and making a million mistakes. In the meantime I was covered with spit and the audience was throwing everything on me.'

Dee Dee's leaving was just another obstacle. It was always this way, always something thrown at us. You just gotta press on. And C.J. was like a young Dee Dee. He was ready for Vietnam – our version of Vietnam. *Joey Ramone*

Whatever C.J. may have lacked in technique and stagecraft, he more than compensated for with exuberance. 'He smiled more during one gig than all the others had during their whole career,' Monte Melnick confirmed. For C.J.'s new brudders, such positivism was exactly what the doctor ordered. The bassist's induction period was a gruelling tour that took in Britain, New Zealand, Australia, Germany, Belgium and Holland. He settled in well, inheriting Dee Dee's vocal duties on songs such as 'Wart Hog'.

'He's great,' enthused Johnny. 'I think the whole thing is that everyone's getting along good – we're all friends. There's less pressure of having to deal with people who are being difficult . . . I'm having more fun now than ever.' 'C.J. fits in good,' continued Marky. 'He's a good guy. He knows how to tour. He doesn't complain every minute. He doesn't get drunk. He's easy to tell things to. He listens.'

And, of course, all the day-to-day hassles of dealing with a wigged-out junkie had vanished. As Joey asserted, 'It's a lot easier to tour now with Dee Dee not with us, because there was too much tension before . . . For a while with Dee Dee it was very rough. It wasn't much fun, there was always some shit going on, some unpleasantness, especially towards the end. Now it's gone and things couldn't be better. It's all very spirited.'

'I guess I contribute what almost any new member of a band contributes – new life,'

Loco Live *(1992) was released thirteen years after the Ramones' previous live album,* It's Alive.

C.J. conceded with enthusiasm. 'I've always perceived the Ramones as more like a gang. I think that's what they want to try and get back towards now, because as time goes by you tend to drift. You can never keep things exactly the same, and I think they changed some, maybe a little more than they wanted.'

But, while C.J. provided the Ramones with a fresh impetus, he wasn't equipped to replace Dee Dee as a songwriter. With Joey gradually cleaning up his act, it was unfair to expect the vocalist to carry the sole burden, while Marky and Johnny were hardly prolific contributors. However, there was no immediate pressure to record a new album, and C.J.'s first three years with the band were spent exclusively on the road. Between January 1990 and September 1993 the Ramones circled the globe, playing more than 400 shows and finding huge new audiences in Argentina and Brazil.

'Joey called me from Argentina, and all of a sudden I heard this screaming and yelling,' recalls Charlotte Lesher. 'I said, "What's all that noise?", and he said, "As I'm talking to you, I'm walking past this open window." The kids had collected outside the hotel and every time he passed by the window, they would yell and scream. He said, "It's just like we're the Beatles."'

Sire attempted to compensate for the lack of new output with a pair of compilations, *All the Stuff and More Vols. One/Two*, and a second live album, *Loco Live*. The collections repackaged the band's first four albums, with additional unreleased material dating from the early period. *Loco Live* was a pale shadow of *It's Alive*. 'It's probably the worst Ramones record ever made,' admits C.J. 'We were forced to work with a producer who had no idea what the Ramones should sound like.'

The album was to mark the end of the band's fifteen-year association with Sire, as the group opted to sign with manager Gary Kurfirst's Radioactive label. Seymour Stein was saddened to see them go, and paid unreserved tribute. 'When people look back on Sire, they'll look back at the Ramones, more than artists who sold 50 times the amount of records that they sold. They are beyond a band, they are an institution.'

The rapid rise and fall of grunge had by this time renewed interest in guitar-based rock. With Kurt Cobain (Nirvana), Eddie Vedder (Pearl Jam) and Chris Cornell

(Soundgarden) citing the Ramones as a key influence, a new generation began to discover the band. The old punk militia had long since deserted the barricades, and punk rock was now co-opted as an element of the diversifying metal scene. Musicians like Metallica's Kirk Hamett were quick to praise the Ramones, previously vilified or ignored by an older generation of headbangers because 'they were so ahead of their time.'

Encouraged by their rising stock, the band began 1992 by cutting their first studio album in three years – *Mondo Bizarro*. Under instructions from Kurfirst to give the album a more contemporary (and more commercial) sound, Ed Stasium was reunited with the band for the first time in nearly eight years.

Also back in touch was Dee Dee, who contributed three songs co-written with Daniel Rey: 'Poison Heart', 'Strength To Endure' and 'Main Man'. Although the group welcomed their former bassist's creative input, they were keeping him at arm's length. 'At this point no one wants him back in the Ramones,' stated Joey.

It was a wise move – cast out from da brudderhood, Dee Dee had initially relocated to Paris with a view to forming a new band with über-junkies Johnny Thunders, ex-Dead Boy Stiv Bators and former Damned guitarist Brian James. Profoundly doomed from the start, the project unravelled almost immediately, leaving Dee Dee wandering destitute in Paris and London. Eventually, he returned to the US desperate to clean up his act. Frosty relations were re-established via Daniel Rey, and Dee Dee was engaged as a songwriter. However, this was by no means a prodigal return – following a drug bust, Dee Dee needed some fast cash. The Ramones bailed him out, but at a price.

'I sold the publishing rights to "Poison Heart", "Main Man" and "Strength To Endure" for a few thousand dollars so I could hire a lawyer to get out of jail,' Dee Dee reflected aloud. The Ramones' lack of sympathy stemmed from his sudden departure. As photographer Bob Gruen explained, 'Dee Dee had left on his own, they didn't have to take him back. And they didn't want to. They just felt that he had dropped them flat, he had left them in the middle of a tour and cost them all a lot of money, without seeming to care.'

1993's Mondo Bizarro *hardly dented the Billboard Top 200.*

Without Dee Dee around, the atmosphere at the *Mondo Bizarro* sessions approached civility. Featuring additional guitar from Rey, former Dictator Andy Shernoff and Living Colour axe-man Vernon Reid, the album also included keyboards by former Psychedelic Fur Joe McGinty on an uninspired cover of the Doors' 'Take It As It Comes'.

Joey contributed seven songs, most notably the anti-PMRC 'Censorshit' and the surf-rock pastiche 'Touring', for which the band were joined by former Turtles Flo and Eddie (Mark Volman and Howard Kaylan) on backing vocals. Marky, writing with partner Skinny Bones, contributed 'Anxiety' and the aptly-titled 'The Job That Ate My Brain'.

Mondo Bizarro featured songs by troubled Dee Dee, no longer a Ramone.

The album gives the impression of the Ramones seeking to recapture themselves. It's apparent in Joey and Daniel Rey's 'Heidi Is A Headcase', which extends the 'Suzy'/'Judy'/'Sheena' lineage. Stasium's sympathetic production was also a key factor, making only superficial attempts at venturing outside traditional Ramones territory.

The Ramones had continuity and credibility. We maintained our self-respect. We did what we wanted to do. *Joey Ramone*

The only incongruity was C.J.'s vocal style. Despite being born in Long Island, and having a Queens background, he simply didn't sound like a Ramone. And the album barely rippled the *Billboard* 200, hitting number 190 before fading away, and the Ramones, once again, returned to the van.

In the spring of 1993, the Ramones returned to New York's Baby Monster studio to record an album of cover versions. The concept certainly had possibilities, the band's influences and reference points providing a wealth of potential material. But anyone expecting an collection of surf/bubblegum/garage punk standards, thrashed to within an inch of their lives, was to be disappointed.

Produced quickly and cheaply with a view to attracting airplay, the album failed miserably to live up to expectations. Unable to wring any commerciality from Ed Stasium, manager and executive producer Gary Kurfirst installed the largely unknown Scott Hackwith as producer. Obviously influenced by Kurfirst's radio-friendly vision of the band, Hackwith's production did nothing to raise the record above the mediocre.

Entitled *Acid Eaters*, the album homed in on the psychedelic era and featured Love,

A good idea poorly executed the 1994 covers album **Acid Eaters.**

Jefferson Airplane, Who and Troggs covers. No Ronettes, no Beach Boys, no Stooges. The album's one surf-song, Jan and Dean's 'Surf City', failed to live up to expectations, lost in the blandness of Hackworth's production and the band's apparent ennui. Joe McGinty provided more unnecessary keyboard noodlings, while Pete Townshend added backing vocals to 'Substitute'.

The tone of the project was set by the hiring of another Kurfirst client, former porn actress Traci Lords, to play the part of Grace Slick on 'Somebody To Love'. As a vocalist, Lords made an outstanding porn star. C.J.'s vocals on 'Journey To The Centre Of The Mind' were only marginally better. 'It was just horrible,' admitted the bassist. *Acid Eaters* lacked inspiration, humour and commercial appeal. It fared only slightly better than *Mondo Bizarro*, climbing to number 179.

Going on the road is touring for the record and making some money. Changing schedules so we could get to the place fast enough to see a baseball game. *Johnny Ramone*

The endless touring resumed, but the band seemed to be going through the motions. Aside from in South America, where they had established a huge fan base, crowds were on the wane. Venues got smaller, as they slipped down the bill at festivals and bigger shows. It was almost as if they were becoming a Ramones tribute act.

Published in June 1993, Jim Bessman's biography, *Ramones: An American Band*, presented an iconic portrait with the co-operation of the band themselves. This arrangement failed to prevent legal hassles relating to reproduction of their lyrics, nor did it delight Dee Dee.

'I told [Bessman] to go fuck himself, y'know, when that book came out,' he seethed, 'running me down like that, putting my ex-wife in there to comment on me – that bitter thing. Saying there was nothing wrong with Phil Spector.'

In February 1994, the Ramones played their 2000th concert in Tokyo, to a large and enthusiastic audience. It was nearly twenty years since they had walked off the streets of Forest Hills and kick-started punk rock. The numerological significance was not lost on Johnny.

'So you had to keep playing because there was nothing else you knew how to do and that was your career,' he observed. 'At the fifteen-year mark I thought it would be really great to reach twenty years and stop . . . So as we reached the twenty-year mark we were doing *Acid Eaters*. I said, "All right, we'll do a Ramones album, stopping after another album. I've had enough."'

We try to maintain what the Ramones are known for – hard, fast, crazy music. *Joey Ramone*

With plenty of touring commitments ahead of them, the band soldiered on throughout the remainder of 1994, supporting metal behemoths Sepultura in South America before huge, delirious crowds. 'We're massive over there,' emphasised Joey. 'The kids over there are very passionate and they love the Ramones . . .'

Dee Dee also experienced some South American passion of his own. In November 1994 he met his second wife, Barbara Zampini, in Buenos Aires. 26 years Dee Dee's junior, Barbara, a huge Ramones fan, would marry her hero two years later when she was eighteen.

With Johnny looking forward to his retirement, Joey recovered from his addictions and embracing a very un-Ramonic health food diet, and Marky and C.J. enjoying touring, an atmosphere of calm professionalism surrounded the peripatetic quartet.

It was during this winding-down period, however, that Joey was diagnosed as suffering from incurable lymphatic cancer. Although his

On the road to extinction? **Adios Amigos** *was the Ramones' final studio album.*

illness was kept secret within the band, it was soon announced that the Ramones would release their final studio album, perform a final tour, and then split. Fittingly, the album was called *Adios Amigos*.

Once again recorded at Baby Monster studios, *Adios* was assisted by Daniel Rey as producer. Having struggled manfully with the patchwork *Animal Boy*, it was fitting that, as a Ramones insider, he was selected for their swansong.

They're the daddy punk group of all time. *Joe Strummer*

Evidence of Joey's fragility was provided by four tracks featuring C.J.'s sincere-yet-bland vocals: of these, 'The Crusher' is a reworking of a Dee Dee song from *Standing In The Spotlight*, while 'Got A Lot To Say' and 'Scattergun' were C.J.'s own compositions.

Joey contributed only two songs – both, viewed in the context of his illness, particularly poignant. His sensitive delivery on 'She Talks To Rainbows' is an exemplar of Joey's vocal style, while the simple lyrics of 'Life's A Gas' can't fail to bring a lump to the throat of any Ramones fan: 'Don't be sad at all . . .'

His vocal on the album's opener, Tom Waits and Kathleen Brennan's 'I Don't Want To Grow Up', is equally affecting. Dee Dee was again in evidence, contributing to six songs including 'Cretin Family', which examines his relationship with the band in

The final Ramones line-up depicted as Mexican bandits – from the Adios Amigos *CD.*

appropriately dumb style, and is only partially ruined by C.J.'s 'Oi, Oi, Oi"'s.

The final track of the final Ramones album is a Stooges-like romp, 'Born To Die In Berlin'. Written by Dee Dee, the song features a vocal by the departed bassist – albeit in German. It didn't signify a reconciliation, but it was a fitting way for the band to go out.

By now, Johnny was no longer bothered about sales. 'It was better when we didn't care if the records would sell and just made them for our fans,' he admitted. '*Adios Amigos*, after 22 years, I think was a very good album. We didn't worry about the hits. I tried never to worry about it after the first three albums. I knew we were going to be a cult band and it was going to stay like that.'

Adios Amigos received an affectionately positive response in the press, and sold better than the band's two previous studio offerings (although it still only reached number 148). Although most reviews chose to focus upon the band's past glories, *Rolling Stone*'s Matt Diehl put it into context: 'The album contains some of their angriest, most powerful material in years, reflecting the alienation of wizened outsiders rather than the snotty adolescent rebellion that had become a Ramones cliché.'

On their final tour, the Ramones were hailed as pioneers by a generation of bands they helped to inspire and who were now sharing the bill with them. Marky, in particular, got a belt out of it: 'Axl Rose of Guns N' Roses and the guys in Pearl Jam wearing our T-shirts. Offspring, Rancid, and Green Day – it was amazing to hear them and definitely hear the big Ramones influence.'

'The true greatness of a band is how many people they've influenced and the Ramones were probably the most influential band of all time,' said C.J., his Johnny-come-lately status stripping his claim of all egotism.

The Ramones finally reached the end of their long, twisted road at the Hollywood Palace, Los Angeles on 6 August 1996. As is often the case with farewell gigs, there was a sense of disappointment that the band were unable to finish on home turf. Despite this, Johnny declared, 'I probably enjoyed my last year more than any other year. But I didn't want to get up there as an ageing rock and roller. 22 years is a long run . . . I know you reach your peak somewhere in your first five years. But I could get up onstage and still feel that we were the best at what we were doing, and I wanted to keep it that way.'

Guest appearances by Dee Dee, Lemmy from Motorhead, Soundgarden and Rancid added to the sense of occasion. Rancid front man Tim Armstrong spoke for many, when he paid tribute to the band's blue-collar trash-punk roots: 'I'm from a low income family. The Ramones, it was my band.'

Farewells, however, were a little premature. Having completed their final tour and quietly dissolved, the Ramones were recommended by Soundgarden for a place on the 1996 Lollapalooza tour. 'We were gonna stop in South America,' recalls Johnny. 'The asshole who runs Lollapalooza comes over and says, "I'm the one who got you on Lollapalooza." I go, ". . . like I give a shit. Our career is over. I'm done. I'm retiring in two more weeks. This makes a difference to me now? Where were you the last six years?'

Despite Johnny's prickly attitude, the festival booking allowed the luxury of an extended goodbye. Additional shows were booked and dates in the US were followed by

tours of Britain and Europe – although some Italian dates were cancelled as Joey's health deteriorated. After a series of shows in New York, the band returned to South America for the final time.

The post-grunge return to prominence of rock music had given rise to a plethora of sub-genres: alt-rock, nu-metal, So-Cal, Brit-pop, all displayed influences derived from the Ramones. Punk rock had finally reached the American mainstream, twenty years after they first took it to Britain. In a sense, the Ramones' unyielding commitment to playing the length and breadth of the USA had finally paid off. Middle America belat-edly recognised their worth. Such acceptance made it a strange time for the band to quit.

As Tommy Erdelyi observed, 'I think they could go on . . . A lot of young people haven't even seen them yet and I think what they should do is take a long rest and then go back on the road . . . There was never anything like the Ramones before. It was a new way of looking at music. It took the rock sound into a psychotic world and narrowed it down into a straight line of energy.'

But Johnny was happy to call it a day, and maintained that the band's current fash-ionable status mattered little. 'Our popularity remained pretty much the same through-out. We made more money each year. And there was no question of slipping in popu-larity.' But still, he admitted, 'I always dwell on the fact that we could have been better. But I feel the Ramones were the most influential American rock band. And that's pret-ty good.'

Even at the very end, despite the in-fighting, the drugs, the endless hours travelling to obscure venues in out-of-the way places, and, ultimately, facing his own mortality, Joey remained irrepressibly upbeat: 'The Ramones were, and are, a great fuckin' band. In spite of our differences. When we went out there to play, the power was intense, like going to see the Who in the Sixties – that intensity and excitement.'

'Don't worry about me.' Joey contemplates life outside of da brudderhood.

Two legends – one hairstyle: Ronnie Spector and Joey Ramone, 1997.

American Zeitgeist

A Ramones story can't really have a happy ending.

Dee Dee Ramone

Having said their protracted goodbyes, the former Ramones went their separate ways. Johnny relocated to Los Angeles to watch baseball, collect Elvis memorabilia and hang out with Eddie Vedder. The band's erstwhile sergeant major had no desire to continue playing, and bequeathed all his Ramones ephemera: 'Daniel Rey's got the Mosrite . . . Eddie [Vedder]'s got the Pinhead, the backdrop. . . . I'm perfectly content with retirement,' continued Johnny. 'In the summer, I'll watch the Yankees game every day. I'll watch a movie or two. I go out to dinner just about every night with my wife . . . I'll sit by the pool.'

When his health allowed, Joey still immersed himself in the New York music scene: organising gigs, producing an EP for Ronnie Spector, hosting a radio show. Marky and C.J. formed new bands and returned to the road.

There was no shortage of published memoirs. The first was Legs McNeil and Gillian McCain's oral history of US punk, *Please Kill Me*, which was published as the band was dissolving. Containing quotes from most of the major mid-Seventies players, it provides an entertainingly candid account of the scene.

Typical is Linda Stein's description of the Ramones bassist: 'The great thing about Dee Dee is that he slept with everybody. Dee Dee slept with me, Dee Dee slept with Seymour, I think he slept with Danny – I mean Dee Dee slept with everybody and anybody. And he made you feel good. I mean, he was a professional hooker!'

Although quoted prominently, Dee Dee was as disgruntled by McNeil's book as he had been with Jim Bessman's: 'He [Mc Neil] was a total asshole . . . A lot of the things he says are off-the-wall, and the people he interviewed are crazy too; Johnny Thunders never hit me over the head with a bottle; I never slept with Linda Stein; I could go on and on and on.'

But the Ramones had actively cultivated their own mythology – whether it was by fabricating their names, giving false dates of birth to appear younger, or contriving their image

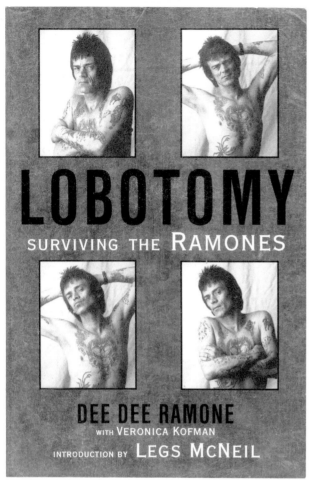

The artist as tattooed love boy – Dee Dee on the cover of his memoir.

as a gang of inseparable brudders. And Dee Dee, as Johnny later contended, was particularly prone to self-mythologising. 'Dee Dee doesn't tell the truth about anything . . . Each person he talks to he gives a totally different story. He had an appendix scar on his stomach. While he was in the band if anybody would ask him he'd tell a story. A knife fight . . . every time a different story.'

Dee Dee was back from an unhappy spell living in Amsterdam, now ensconced in the Chelsea Hotel. (Notorious as the scene where Sid Vicious murdered his girlfriend, former professional groupie Nancy Spungeon.) Looking back on his career as a Ramone, Dee Dee reflected, 'I know how lucky I am. I have my Ramones publishing. I really worked for what I got. I really risked my life for it . . . But I wouldn't recommend it now, 'cos there's just too many ways you could get in trouble, get killed, get hurt, end up on drugs, end up defenceless mentally because you don't form normal defences in life.'

And the past kept on returning, as Radioactive milked the band's legacy for all it was worth. They issued two live albums: 1996's *Greatest Hits Live*, recorded at one of the final New York gigs, and the following year's *We're Outta Here*. Although both albums contained previously unreleased tracks – Motorhead's tribute song 'R.A.M.O.N.E.S.', and a cover of Sixties stompers the Dave Clark Five's 'Any Way You Want It' – neither added anything of worth to the Ramones discography. 'Ultimately, it's the accumulated mass of past glories,' said *Mojo* of *We're Outta Here*, 'rather than anything approaching a life-affirming experience, which keeps the brudders afloat here.'

Irritated by published accounts of his own life story, Dee Dee took a shot at setting the record straight. In 1997 he published *Poison Heart: Surviving the Ramones*, with assistance from writer Veronica Kaufman.

An entertaining, if whiny, read, *Poison Heart* revealed more about the former bassist's erratic mental state than it did about the band's career. Dee Dee relentlessly portrays himself as a victim throughout: 'I was extremely hated. Nobody in my life cared about me.' Later edited by Danny Weizmann and re-issued as *Lobotomy: Surviving the Ramones*, the new edition featured an introduction by 'total asshole' Legs McNeil.

Described by Phil Sutcliffe in *Q* as 'the true, pathetic, awesome voice of the Ramones,' neither version found great favour with his former compadres. 'Dee Dee was my best friend, but he fantasised a lot, which made him a great writer,' revealed Marky. 'A lot of the stuff in his two books is 75 per cent fact and 25 per cent imagination. I knew him so well that I could pinpoint the stuff that wasn't real.'

Britney Spears? I wouldn't go out with her. You think her mother would like me? *Dee Dee Ramone*

'In his book there ain't gonna be nothing that was really gonna be true except his warped, crazy view of things,' agreed Johnny.

But, despite his continuing struggle with addiction, Dee Dee became an addled Renaissance man. He produced (very) primitive art, published his own fanzine (about the wonderful world of Dee Dee and his favourite things), and formed the Remainz – an occasional band that also included Marky, and performed selections from the Ramones catalogue. In their latter days, half of the Ramones had become their own tribute band.

Further establishing himself as punk rock's Walter Mitty, Dee Dee harnessed his imagination to write a novel, *Chelsea Horror Hotel*, published in 2001. It spectacularly blurred the distinctions between the writer's life and his fantasies, featuring the weird inhabitants and environment of the notorious junkie locale.

'It's kind of the way it feels, living there,' claimed Dee Dee. 'It's a very eerie place. And it's always had a lot of paranormal experiences there. It's got that kind of atmosphere. Just the architecture alone is kind of conducive to, y'know, mystery. The chaos of living on 23rd Street is a story in itself.'

As with his autobiographical works, Dee Dee casts himself as the unfortunate hero beset by all manner of twisted, druggy lunacy:

Dee Dee's primitive painting of the Chelsea Hotel was featured on the cover of his 2001 novel.

A rare shot of Joey and Dee Dee performing together post-Ramones, taken at the Continental Club, New York City, 27 November 1997.

As I reached up both of my arms to grab at the two strange things growing out of my skull, I failed to be aware there was also a tail coming out now – almost fully grown – of my backside. A kind of devil tail with a forked end . . . I was trying to reach up and grab the two horns sticking out of my skull . . .

The book features the ghosts of Johnny Thunders, Sid Vicious, Stiv Bators and New York Dolls drummer Jerry Nolan, who join Dee Dee for a basement concert before descending into Hell. The author saw his book as a written extension of the Ramones tradition. 'I'm still writing about lobotomies and "the dope is my friend" . . . it's really crazy stuff. I don't know what's making me feel like that, but it feels like maybe I've done that enough.' Or maybe he'd done it all too much.

Throughout the 1990s, compilation albums continued to re-package both the Ramones' classic recordings and their less vintage tracks. Radioactive released a second volume of *Ramones Mania*, featuring the best of the band's later material, while Warners retaliated with a more fulsome collection, the 57-track double CD *Anthology*, in 1999.

Reviewing *Anthology*, *Trouser Press* journalist Ira Rollins highlighted the band's enduring influence: 'Nobody doesn't like the Ramones. They're as immortal as America's other band, the Beach Boys. Whatever punk became – ruined canvases of

Mohawked body art, hormone-fuelled assholes battering each other senseless in mosh pits, uptight activists barking tuneless ideology to conformist converts, Nazis, anarchists, prim straight-edgers and proto-metal dorks sinking into the post-Sabbath sludge – the Ramones remained its true nucleus.'

But, on Easter Sunday, 15 April 2001, the heart of that nucleus stopped beating. Five weeks shy of his 50th birthday, for which preparations had already been made, Joey Ramone succumbed to his illness. At the end of the previous year, he'd injured his hip in falling on the sidewalk outside his apartment. An operation was required, which meant Joey had to temporarily cease taking the medication that inhibited the spread of cancer. This cessation allowed lymphoma to take a firm grip. Despite hefty doses of steroids and increased chemotherapy, he had faded rapidly.

Joey was great. He was one of the most unusual and most enlightening people I've ever known. Always friendly, always up, no matter what the situation. Fought it to the bitter end, was always happy. I thought he was gonna beat it. Too bad he didn't get to see these [early album reissues] come out. He did get to see his face on the cover of *Spin* magazine. They were never on the cover of *Rolling Stone*. *Ed Stasium*

Joey's gentle, optimistic nature left its mark on all those who knew him or loved his music. 'His family can be very proud of Joey for the person he was,' said Marty Thau, producer of the Ramones' early demos. 'Everyone misses him.' C.J. paid tribute: 'No matter what anybody thinks or no matter what anybody says, Joey was one of the most influential people in rock 'n' roll ever.'

Johnny, however, had been uncomfortable with the idea of visiting Joey in hospital. He'd continued to monitor his former bandmate's condition via regular phone calls to Arturo Vega. Their personal history, and the bad blood between them, had made it impossible for them ever to get close. Even at the end. 'It didn't really sink in until I got home and there was, like, twenty messages,' Johnny lamented. 'After a week of that, I felt very depressed.'

Even after death, however, Dee Dee refused to forgive Joey for snubbing him after he quit the band. 'He wasn't my friend anymore. He didn't like me,' he complained, whining about how he'd always been the band scapegoat. 'He constantly slandered me, put me down, ruined every opportunity he could, selfish as could be, kept everything for himself. They always played me down like I was some helpless lunatic . . . And [the other Ramones] never accomplished anything on their own. Zero . . . After he died, they're having this concert, the Ramones, and I wasn't asked to play!'

After this barrage of vitriol, Marky put things in perspective. 'I was the only Ramone to see him in the hospital and I was the only Ramone who played on his solo album. We were the closest. We fought the most but we made up the most. Johnny and Dee Dee didn't talk to him at all for eighteen years and they never made up, but that's their choice, they had deeper issues.' Strangely, Marky seemed to overlook how, despite being pissed off by Dee Dee bailing out of the band, Joey often gave spirited defences of his wayward brudder.

A posthumous 50th birthday party for Joey, at the Hammerstein Ballroom in Manhattan, was also the venue for more unseemly squabbling. The event was organised by Joey's mother, Charlotte Lesher, and his brother, Mickey Leigh. Marky saw Leigh's involvement as the worst kind of opportunism.

'When Joey died, his mother inherited his estate,' explained the drummer. 'The Ramones were going to play the show, but the brother wanted to sing with us. We wanted Joe Strummer to do it, Rob Zombie, and Eddie Vedder. He insisted that he sing so we told him to go fuck himself, and we didn't go and we told a lot of the other bands not to go or play.'

Leigh may only have wanted to pay homage to his late brother, but the wrangling over who performed served to sour the tribute. More positive was the memorial left by Joey himself – a solo album, poignantly entitled *Don't Worry About Me*, issued by Sanctuary Records in February 2002.

Joey's posthumously released solo album, 2001.

Accompanied throughout by Daniel Rey on guitar and Andy Shernoff on bass, the album also features Marky on six of the eleven tracks. Other guests include Joe McGinty, who had provided keyboards for *Mondo Bizarro* and *Acid Eaters*, Mickey Leigh, and Damned guitarist Captain Sensible. Given the personnel, it's unsurprising that *Don't Worry About Me* sounds pretty much like a Ramones album. Aside from its single, a heart-rending cover of 'What A Wonderful World' (beginning with a similar intro to the Sex Pistols' 'Pretty Vacant'), and a version of the Stooges' '1969', Joey con-

The Ramones take their rightful place in the Rock & Roll Hall Of Fame, March 2002 (Dee Dee, Johnny, Tommy, Marky).

tributed all the songs.

Particularly emotional are 'Stop Thinking About It' and 'I Got Knocked Down (But I'll Get Up)', as they address the vocalist's struggle to overcome his illness, while the title track showcases his voice to good effect. *Don't Worry About Me* stands as a powerful tribute to its maker, the back cover of the liner booklet depicting an impromptu shrine to Joey built by his fans.

One month later, the Ramones were inducted into the Rock & Roll Hall of Fame – an imminent event the ailing Joey had been aware of, but felt was of no personal significance. Once again, trouble kicked off.

'Dee Dee didn't want to be around John and no one had really seen Tommy [on a social basis] since 1977,' insisted Marky. 'I dedicated my award to Charlotte and Mickey, Joey's mother and brother, since Joey was gone. They didn't want Charlotte and Mickey up there . . . Johnny even came up to me and asked me to stop kissing Charlotte and Mickey's ass. I told him if I wasn't at the Hall of Fame I'd take him outside and kick the shit out of him.'

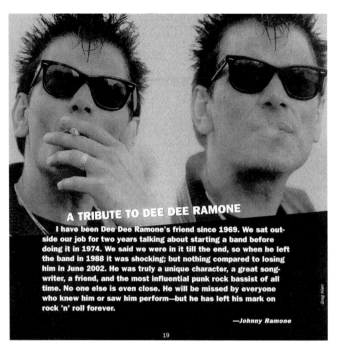

A TRIBUTE TO DEE DEE RAMONE

I have been Dee Dee Ramone's friend since 1969. We sat outside our job for two years talking about starting a band before
doing it in 1974. We said we were in it till the end, so when he left
the band in 1988 it was shocking; but nothing compared to losing
him in June 2002. He was truly a unique character, a great songwriter, a friend, and the most influential punk rock bassist of all
time. No one else is even close. He will be missed by everyone
who knew him or saw him perform—but he has left his mark on
rock 'n' roll forever.

—*Johnny Ramone*

19

A posthumous tribute to Dee Dee, by his estranged brudder Johnny.

Marky was equally annoyed at the organisers' refusal to present C.J. with an award, despite his being with the band for eight years. Dee Dee refused to dress in traditional Ramones costume, turning up in a sharp black suit, while Tommy had aged into a Jerry Garcia lookalike.

It was left to Marty Thau to contextualise the band's significance: 'When the Ramones split up, it was Joey who lent his name to the downtown music scene and assisted many young and aspiring musicians in their pursuit of a contract. When he died, I cried. The Ramones will go down in history for having reintroduced blazing energy and humour into rock 'n' roll – they inspire to this day.'

I don't know if someone put a curse on me the day I was born, or on my mother. But whatever, nothing ever goes right for me. *Dee Dee Ramone*

Within three months of the Hall of Fame ceremony, Dee Dee was dead. His wife, Barbara, discovered his body at their Hollywood apartment on Thursday, 6 June 2002. The cause of his death was immediately identified as a heroin overdose, although official confirmation was not forthcoming for weeks. Given his on-off addiction, and the low tolerance of a cleaned-up junkie who takes up the needle again, it was inevitable.

However, the news came as a shock to Dee Dee's former bandmates, who thought he'd finally overcome his dependency. 'When Dee Dee died it was unexpected since he was clean. I told him anytime he needed someone to talk to I was always available,' said a saddened Marky.

Johnny was equally stunned. 'I saw Dee Dee about two weeks before it happened,' he confirmed. 'I saw him on Hollywood Boulevard. We had spoken a few times. We went out for lunch before the Rock & Roll Hall of Fame [induction ceremony] and I convinced him to go to it . . . there were different periods of time where you could have expected something like this to happen, but Dee Dee was always a survivor and so it came as a shock.'

Dee Dee was the bad boy of the Ramones, and also, nominally, the good-looking one. In the final years of his life, the bassist acquired a menacing demeanour: greying and festooned with tattoos, he lived in the twilight world of an ageing junkie. 'I think that Dee Dee was destined to be a man of the street,' opined Arturo Vega. And so he died as he had lived.

Guess I'll always be a Ramone. *Johnny Ramone*

'I have to say I loved Dee Dee,' asserted photographer Roberta Bayley, 'he was a completely charming and totally exasperating person, two characteristics that are difficult to combine! . . . I think Dee Dee was very creative and very unhappy but he was like a child in his desire to please and his desire to shock . . . No one could make up a person like Dee Dee.'

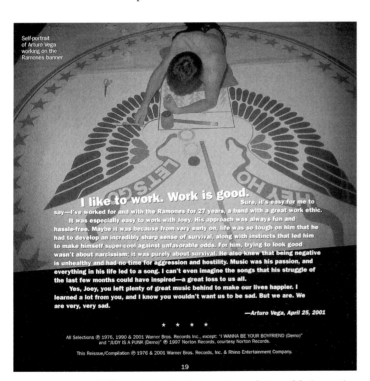

Self-portrait of Arturo Vega working on the Ramones banner

I like to work. Work is good. Sure, it's easy for me to say—I've worked for and with the Ramones for 27 years, a band with a great work ethic. It was especially easy to work with Joey. His approach was always fun and hassle-free. Maybe it was because from very early on, life was so tough on him that he had to develop an incredibly sharp sense of survival, along with instincts that led him to make himself super-cool against unfavorable odds. For him, trying to look good wasn't about narcissism; it was purely about survival. He also knew that being negative is unhealthy and had no time for aggression and hostility. Music was his passion, and everything in his life led to a song. I can't even imagine the songs that his struggle of the last few months could have inspired—a great loss to us all.

Yes, Joey, you left plenty of great music behind to make our lives happier. I learned a lot from you, and I know you wouldn't want us to be sad. But we are. We are very, very sad.

—Arturo Vega, April 25, 2001

★ ★ ★ ★

All Selections ℗ 1976, 1990 & 2001 Warner Bros. Records Inc., except: "I WANNA BE YOUR BOYFRIEND (Demo)" and "JUDY IS A PUNK (Demo)" ℗ 1997 Norton Records, courtesy Norton Records.

This Reissue/Compilation ℗ 1976 & 2001 Warner Bros. Records, Inc. & Rhino Entertainment Company.

19

A tribute to the late Joey by Arturo Vega – designer of the Ramones' American Eagle emblem.

Dee Dee's death ultimately negated any possibility of a Ramones reunion – but, without Joey, it would have been a hollow exercise anyway. Still, rumours persisted, though it was the more realistic prospect of a tribute album that soon came to pass.

'I was approached about it and I said, "Yeah I'll be involved but I have to have full say,"' confirmed former group leader Johnny. 'They said, "Yeah fine." So I said, "I can get Eddie Vedder, I can get Rob Zombie and I can get the Chili Peppers and Marilyn Manson and Metallica."'

With partial profits going to the Lymphoma Research Foundation, based in New York City, *We're A Happy Family – A Tribute To The*

Ramones was issued by Columbia in February 2003. The album's promotional literature featured the following accolade from Rob Zombie, who contributed a version of 'Blitzkrieg Bop': 'The Ramones are in my opinion the greatest American rock band. For over two decades they remained true to everything that rock 'n' roll needs to be – loud, fast and stripped down to the core. The Ramones will forever be cemented in my brain as four teenage punks in black leather and blue jeans ready to crack your skull with a baseball bat.'

Besides the artists already mentioned, *We're A Happy Family* also featured covers by U2 (fittingly as, Joey had been listening to the band on his sickbed), KISS, the Pretenders, Rancid, Garbage, Green Day, the Offspring and Tom Waits. Tribute albums tend to be lacklustre affairs, but it was a tribute in itself that such a range of high-profile performers turned up. Greeted by mixed reviews, *We're A Happy Family* is best viewed as a mark of respect to a band that forever influenced the shape and form of rock music.

Over 22 years, the Ramones released fourteen studio albums (at least three of which are absolute classics), played 2,263 shows, germinated punk rock on both sides of the Atlantic, and influenced generations of bands to return to simple, no-frills rock 'n' roll. As Joey once put it, 'Not bad for a bunch of half-wits, huh?'

Selected discography

Studio Albums

Ramones
released **April 1976**
(Sire SASD 7250)

Joey Ramone (vocals) – Dee Dee Ramone (bass) – Johnny Ramone (guitar) – Tommy Ramone (drums)
Producer: **Craig Leon**

Fourteen tracks: *Blitzkreig Bop/Beat On The Brat/Judy Is A Punk/I Wanna Be Your Boyfriend/ Chainsaw/Now I Wanna Sniff Some Glue/I Don't Wanna Go Down To The Basement/Loudmouth/Havana Affair/Listen To My Heart/53rd & 3rd/Let's Dance/I Don't Wanna Walk Around With You/Today Your Love Tomorrow The World*

Leave Home
released **January 1977** (Sire SA7528)

Joey Ramone (vocals) – Dee Dee Ramone (bass) – Johnny Ramone (guitar) – Tommy Ramone (drums)
Producers: **Tony Bongiovi and Tommy Erdelyi**

Fourteen tracks: *Glad To See You Go/Gimme Gimme Shock Treatment/ I Remember You/Oh Oh, I Love Her So/Carbona Not Glue*/Suzy Is A Headbanger/Pinhead/Now I Wanna Be A Good Boy/Swallow My Pride/ What's Your Game?/California Sun/ Commando/You're Gonna Kill That Girl/You Should Never Have Opened That Door*

*Carbona Not Glue replaced by Sheena Is A Punk Rocker on later US pressings, Babysitter in the UK.

Rocket To Russia
released **November 1977** (Sire SR 6042)

Joey Ramone (vocals) – Dee Dee Ramone (bass) – Johnny Ramone (guitar) – Tommy Ramone (drums)
Producers: **Tony Bongiovi and Tommy Erdelyi**

Fourteen tracks: *Cretin Hop/ Rockaway Beach/Here Today, Gone Tomorrow/Locket Love/I Don't Care/Sheena Is A Punk Rocker/We're A Happy Family/Teenage Lobotomy/ Do You Wanna Dance?/I Wanna Be Well/I Can't Give You Anything/ Ramona/Surfin' Bird/Why Is It Always This Way?*

Road To Ruin
released **September 1978**
(Sire SRK 6063)

Joey Ramone (vocals) – Dee Dee Ramone (bass) – Johnny Ramone (guitar) – Marky Ramone (drums)
Producers: **Tommy Erdelyi and Ed Stasium**

Twelve tracks: *I Just Want To Have Something To Do/I Wanted Everything/Don't Come Close/I Don't Want You/Needles And Pins/ I'm Against It/I Wanna Be Sedated/Go Mental/Questioningly/ She's The One/Bad Brain/It's A Long Way Back*

End Of The Century
released **January 1980**
(Sire SRK 6077)

Joey Ramone (vocals) – Dee Dee Ramone (bass) – Johnny Ramone (guitar) – Marky Ramone (drums)

Producer: **Phil Spector**
Twelve tracks: *Do You Remember Rock 'N' Roll Radio?/I'm Affected/Danny Says/Chinese Rock/The Return Of Jackie And Judy/Let's Go/Baby I Love You/I Can't Make It On Time/This Ain't Havana/Rock 'n' Roll High School/ All The Way/High Risk Insurance*

Pleasant Dreams
released **July 1981**
(Sire SRK 3571)

Joey Ramone (vocals) – Dee Dee Ramone (bass) – Johnny Ramone (guitar) – Marky Ramone (drums)
Producer: **Graham Gouldman**

Twelve tracks: *We Want The Airwaves/All's Quiet On The Eastern Front/The KKK Took My Baby Away/Don't Go/You Sound Like You're Sick/It's Not My Place (In The 9 To 5 World)/She's A Sensation/7-11/You Didn't Mean Anything To Me/Come On Now/This Business Is Killing Me/Sitting In My Room*

Subterranean Jungle
released **February 1983**
(Sire 7 23800-1)

Joey Ramone (vocals) – Dee Dee Ramone (bass) – Johnny Ramone

(guitar) – Marky Ramone (drums)
Producers: **Ritchie Cordell and Glen Kolotkin**

Twelve tracks: *Little Bit O' Soul/I Need Your Love/Outsider/What'd Ya Do?/Highest Trails Above/Somebody Like Me/Psycho Therapy/Time Has Come Today/My-My Kind Of Girl/In The Park/Time Bomb/Every Time I Eat Vegetables It Makes Me Think Of You*

Too Tough To Die
released **October 1984**
(Sire 7 25817-1)

Joey Ramone (vocals) – Dee Dee Ramone (bass) – Johnny Ramone (guitar) – Richie Ramone (drums)
Producers: **Tommy Erdelyi and Ed Stasium**

Thirteen tracks: *Mama's Boy/I'm Not Afraid Of Life/Too Tough To Die/Durango 95/Wart Hog/Danger Zone/Chasing The Night/Howling At The Moon/Daytime Dilemma (Dangers Of Love)/Planet Earth 1988/Human Kind/Endless Vacation/No Go*

Animal Boy
released **May 1986**
(Sire 7-25433-1)

Joey Ramone (vocals) – Dee Dee Ramone (bass) – Johnny Ramone (guitar) – Richie Ramone (drums)
Producer: **Jean Beauvoir**

Twelve tracks: *Somebody Put Something In My Drink/Animal Boy/Love Kills/Apeman Hop/She Belongs To Me/Crummy Stuff/My Brain Is Hanging Upside Down (Bonzo Goes To Bitburg)/Mental Hell/Eat That Rat/Freak Of Nature/Hair Of The Dog/Something To Believe In*

Halfway To Sanity
released **September 1987**
(Sire 9 25641-1)

Joey Ramone (vocals) – Dee Dee Ramone (bass) – Johnny Ramone (guitar) – Richie Ramone (drums)
Producers: **Daniel Rey and the Ramones**

Twelve tracks: *I Wanna Live/Bop 'Til You Drop/Garden Of Serenity/Weasel Face/Go L'il Camaro Go/I Know Better Now/Death Of Me/I Lost My Mind/A Real Cool Time/I'm Not Jesus/Bye Bye Baby/Worm Man*

Brain Drain
released **May 1989**
(Sire 7 25905-1)

Joey Ramone (vocals) – Dee Dee Ramone (bass) – Johnny Ramone (guitar) – Marky Ramone (drums)
Producer: **Bill Laswell**

Twelve tracks: *I Believe In Miracles/Zero Zero UFO/Don't Bust My Chops/Punishment Fits The Crime/All Screwed Up/Palisades Park/Pet Sematary/Learn To Listen/Can't Get You Outta My Mind/Ignorance Is Bliss/Come Back Baby/Merry Christmas (I Don't Want To Fight Tonight)*

Mondo Bizarro
released **September 1992**
(Radioactive RAR-10615)

Joey Ramone (vocals) – Johnny Ramone (guitar) – C.J. Ramone (bass) – Marky Ramone (drums)
Producer: **Ed Stasium**

Thirteen tracks: *Censorshit/The Job That Ate My Brain/Poison Heart/Anxiety/Strength To Endure/It's Gonna Be Alright/Take It As It Comes/ Main Man/Tomorrow She Goes Away/I Won't Let It Happen/Cabbies On Crack/Heidi Is A Headcase/Touring*

Acid Eaters
released **May 1993**
(Chrysalis CHR 6052)

Joey Ramone (vocals) – Johnny Ramone (guitar) – C.J. Ramone (bass) – Marky Ramone (drums)
Producer: **Scott Hackwith**

Twelve tracks: *Journey To The Center Of The Mind/ Substitute/Out Of Time/The Shape Of Things To Come/Somebody To Love/When I Was Young/Seven And Seven Is/My Back Pages/Can't Seem To Make You Mine/Have You Ever Seen The Rain?/I Can't Control Myself/Surf City*

Adios Amigos
released **April 1995**
(Radioactive RARD-11273)

Joey Ramone (vocals) – Johnny Ramone (guitar) – C.J. Ramone (bass) – Marky Ramone (drums)
Producer: **Daniel Rey**

Thirteen tracks: *I Don't Wanna Grow Up/Makin' Monsters For My Friend/It's Not For Me To Know/The Crusher/Life's A Gas/Take The Pain Away/I Love You/Cretin Family/Have A Nice Day/Scatter-gun/Got A Lot To Say/She Talks To Rainbows/Born To Die In Berlin*

Live Albums

It's Alive
released **April 1979**
(Sire/Warner SRK2-6074)

Joey Ramone (vocals) – Dee Dee Ramone (bass) – Johnny Ramone

(guitar) – Tommy Ramone (drums)
Producers: **Tommy Erdelyi and Ed Stasium**

28 tracks: *Rockaway Beach/Teenage Lobotomy/Blitzkrieg Bop/I Wanna Be Well/Glad To See You Go/Gimme Gimme Shock Treatment/You're Gonna Kill That Girl/I Don't Care/ Sheena Is A Punk Rocker/Havana Affair/Commando/Here Today, Gone Tomorrow/Surfin' Bird/Cretin Hop/ Listen To My Heart/California Sun/ I Don't Wanna Walk Around With You/Pinhead/Do You Wanna Dance?/Chainsaw/Today Your Love, Tomorrow The World/I Wanna Be A Good Boy/Judy Is A Punk/Suzy Is A Headbanger/Let's Dance/Oh Oh I Love Her So/Now I Wanna Sniff Some Glue/We're A Happy Family* Recorded at the Rainbow Theatre, London, December 1977

Loco Live
released **March 1992**
(Sire/Warner 9-26650-2)

Joey Ramone (vocals) – Johnny Ramone (guitar) – C.J. Ramone (bass) – Marky Ramone (drums)
Producers: **Adam Yellin and the Ramones**

32 tracks: *The Good, The Bad And The Ugly/ Durango 95/Teenage Lobotomy/Psycho Therapy/Blitzkrieg Bop/Do You Remember Rock 'N' Roll Radio?/I Believe In Miracles/ Gimme Gimme Shock Treatment/ Rock 'N' Roll High School/I Wanna Be Sedated/The KKK Took My Baby Away/I Wanna Live/My Brain Is Hanging Upside Down (Bonzo Goes To Bitburg)/Chinese Rock/Sheena Is A Punk Rocker/Rockaway Beach/Pet Sematary/Judy Is A Punk/Mamma's Boy/Animal Boy/Wart Hog/Surfin' Bird/Cretin Hop/I Don't Wanna Walk Around With You/Today Your*

Love, Tomorrow The World/ Pinhead/Somebody Put Something In My Drink/Beat On The Brat/ Ignorance Is Bliss/I Just Want To Have Something To Do/Havana Affair/I Don't Wanna Go Down To The Basement
Recorded in Barcelona, Spain, April 1991

Greatest Hits Live
released **June 1996**
(Radioactive RARD–11459-A)

Joey Ramone (vocals) – Johnny Ramone (guitar) – C.J. Ramone (bass) – Marky Ramone (drums)
Producers: **Ed Stasium and Daniel Rey**

Eighteen tracks: *Durango 95/ Blitzkrieg Bop/Do You Remember Rock 'N' Roll Radio?/I Wanna Be Sedated/Spiderman/I Don't Want To Grow Up/Sheena Is A Punk Rocker/ Rockaway Beach/Strength To Endure/Cretin Family/Do You Wanna Dance?/We're A Happy Family/The Crusher/53rd & 3rd/ Beat On The Brat/Pet Sematary/ R.A.M.O.N.E.S.*/Any Way You Want It**
Recorded at the Academy, New York, February 1996

* Additional studio recordings

We're Outta Here!
released **November 1997**
(Radioactive RARD-11555)

Joey Ramone (vocals) – Johnny Ramone (guitar) – C.J. Ramone (bass) – Marky Ramone (drums)
Plus Guests : Dee Dee Ramone/ Chris Cornell and Ben Shepherd (Soundgarden)/Lemmy Kilmeister (Motorhead)/Tim Armstrong and Lars Fredericksen (Rancid)/Eddie

Vedder (Pearl Jam)
Producer: **Daniel Rey**
32 tracks: *Durango 95/Teenage Lobotomy/Psycho Therapy/Blitzkrieg Bop/Do You Remember Rock 'N' Roll Radio?/I Believe In Miracles/ Gimme Gimme Shock Treatment/ Rock 'N' Roll High School/I Wanna Be Sedated/Spiderman/The KKK Took My Baby Away/I Just Want To Have Something To Do/Commando/ Sheena Is A Punk Rocker/Rockaway Beach/Pet Sematary/The Crusher/ Love Kills/Do You Wanna Dance?/ Somebody Put Something In My Drink/I Don't Want You/Wart Hog/ Cretin Hop/R.A.M.O.N.E.S./Today Your Love, Tomorrow The World/ Pinhead/53rd & 3rd/Listen To My Heart/We're A Happy Family/ Chinese Rock/Beat On The Brat/Any Way You Want It*
Recorded at the Palace, Los Angeles, August 1996

Compilation Albums

All The Stuff And More Volume One
(Sire 7599-26220-1) **1990**
33 tracks

All The Stuff And More Volume Two
(Sire 9-26618-2) **1991**
30 tracks

Ramones Mania
(Sire 9 25709-1) **1998**
30 tracks

Ramones Mania Two
(Toshiba EMI TOCP-65233) **1999**
25 tracks – Japanese release

Hey Ho, Let's Go!! Ramones Anthology *(Rhino/Warner R2 75817)* **1999**
58 tracks

Best Of The Chrysalis Years
(EMI 5-38472-2) **2002**
Eighteen tracks

The Chrysalis Years Anthology
(EMI 541080-2) **2002**
84 tracks

Singles

Blitzkreig Bop/Havana Affair
(Sire SAA 725) **1976**

**I Wanna Be Your Boyfriend/
California Sun/I Don't Wanna
Walk Around With You**
(Sire SAA 734) **1976**

Swallow My Pride/Pinhead
(Sire SA 738) **1977**

**Sheena Is A Punk Rocker/I Don't
Care**
(Sire SA 746) **1977**

Rockaway Beach/Locket Love
(Sire SRE 1008) **1977**

**Do You Wanna Dance?/
Babysitter**
(Sire SRE 1017) **1977**

**Don't Come Close/I Don't Want
You**
(Sire SRE 1025) **1978**

**Needles And Pins/I Wanted
Everything**
(Sire SRE 1045) **1978**

**Rock 'n' Roll High School/Do
You Wanna Dance?**
(Sire SRE 1051) **1979**

**Baby I Love You/High Risk
Insurance**
(Sire SRE 49182) **1980**

**Do You Remember Rock 'n' Roll
Radio?/Let's Go**
(Sire SRE 49261) **1980**

**We Want The Airwaves/All's
Quiet On The Eastern Front**
(Sire SRE 49812) **1981**

**Time Has Come Today/Psycho
Therapy**
(Sire W9606) *1983

Howling At The Moon/Smash You
(Beggars Banquet BEG 128) *1985

**Bonzo Goes To Bitburg/Daytime
Dilemma (Dangers Of Love)**
(Beggars Banquet BEG 140) *1985

**Somebody Put Something In My
Drink/Something To Believe In**
(Beggars Banquet BEG 157) *1986

Crummy Stuff/She Belongs To Me
(Beggars Banquet BEG 167) *1986

Real Cool Time/Life Goes On
(Beggars Banquet BEG 198) *1987

**I Wanna Live/Merry Christmas (I
Don't Want To Fight Tonight)**
(Beggars Banquet BEG 201) *1987

**I Wanna Be Sedated/I Wanna Be
Sedated (Mega Mix)**
(Sire 9 27663-7) **1988**

**Pet Sematary/Sheena Is A Punk
Rocker**
(Sire 9 22911-7) **1989**

Poison Heart/Censorshit
(Chrysalis CHS 3917) * **1992**
*UK release only

Selected Solo Albums

**Dee Dee King: Standing In The
Spotlight**
released **March 1989**
(Sire 1-25884)
Producer: **Daniel Rey**

Ten tracks: *Mashed Potato Time/2
Much 2 Drink/Baby Doll/Poor Little
Rich Girl/Commotion In The Ocean/
German Kid/Brooklyn Babe/
Emergency/The Crusher/I Want
What I Want When I Want It*

**Joey Ramone: Don't Worry
About Me**
released **February 2002**
(Sanctuary BO0OO5V62X)
Producer: **Daniel Rey**

Eleven tracks: *What A Wonderful
World/Stop Thinking About It/Mr.
Punchy/Maria Bartiromo/Spirit In
My House/Venting/Like A Drug I
Never Did Before/Searching For
Something/I Got Knocked Down
(But I'll Get Up)/1969/Don't Worry
About Me*

Acknowledgements

Putting together *A Complete Twisted History* entailed a wide ranging exploration of the music media. Books that were particularly useful included; Antonia, Nina *Johnny Thunders: In Cold Blood* (Cherry Red Books 2000); Bessman, Jim *Ramones – An American Band* (Saint Martin's Press 1993); Gimarc, George *Punk Diary 1970-79* (Vintage/Random House 1994); Heylin, Clinton *From The Velvets To The Voidoids: A Pre-Punk History For The Post Punk World* (Penguin, 1993); Holmstrom, John *Punk: The Original* (US, High Times 1998); McNeil, Legs & McCain, Gillian *Please Kill Me: The Uncensored Oral History of Punk* (US 1996, Grove Press); Monk, Noel E & Guterman, Jimmy *12 Days On The Road – The Sex Pistols and America* (US, William Morrow 1990); Perry, Mark *The Bible – Sniffin' Glue...* (UK Michael Dempsey 1978); Ramone, Dee Dee *Chelsea Horror Hotel* (US, Thunder's Mouth Press 2001); Ramone, Dee Dee & Kaufman, Veronica *Lobotomy: Surviving The Ramones* (US, Thunder's Mouth Press 2000); Savage, Jon *England's Dreaming: Sex Pistols and Punk Rock* (UK Faber & Faber 1992); Stevenson, Nils & Stevenson, Ray *Vacant: A Diary of The Punk Years 1976-79* (UK, Thames and Hudson 1999); Vale, V *Search & Destroy: The Authoritative Guide To Punk Culture* (US V/Search Publications 1996).

The following sources have also proven invaluable in the researching of this book; Periodicals – *NME, Sounds, Zigzag, Melody Maker, Q, Mojo, the Guardian, Kerrang!, Punk Magazine, Village Voice, Rolling Stone, Creem.* Websites – *fastnbulbous.com, cbgb.com, deedeeramone.net, ramones.nl, hiljaset.sci.fi/punk.net, joeyramone.com, punk77.co.uk, q4music.com, ramonesonline.com, trashsurfin.de, hemi.passagen.se/ak5/ramones, markperry.freeuk.com, trakmarx.com, rockmine.music.co.uk, artistdirect.com, rockonthenet.com, sing365.com, officialramones.com, www.kauhajoki.fi/~jplaitio/ramones.html, venus.space-ports.com/~ivo/ramones.html, home.i-plus.net/scathach/carbona, joeyramone4ever.homestead.com, ramones-club.de, nyrock.com, ramones.be, dreknik.net/ramone, punkbands.com, swipnet.se/~w-35837/ramones_e.html, mtv.com, littlecrackedegg.com.*

Special thanks to my other half, Donna Greene, for her assistance and endurance. I'd also like to thank my grandparents, Fred and Nin, and my mother, Maureen, for putting up with all that noise for all those years.

The following individuals have provided vital assistance or materials; Adam Ryan, Lisa Watson, Steve Kelly, Chis Asher, Yvette Haynes and special thanks to Kris Needs for the loan of his interview tapes with the Ramones and for allowing us access to his early Ramones newspaper cuttings. I'd like to thank everybody at Plexus: Sandra Wake, Terry Porter, Paul Woods, Chloe Lola Riess, Louise Coe and Rebecca Martin for their high-octane efforts and enthusiasm. Also thanks to Brian Flynn for his designs.

We would like to thank the following photographers and picture agenices for supplying photographs: Sire Records; Michael Putland/Retna; Ebet Roberts/Redferns; Kees Tabak/Sunshine/Retna; Michael Ochs/Retna; Pieter Mazel/Retna; Robert Matheau/Retna; Ian Dickson/Redferns; Adrian Boot/Retna; Barry Schultz/Sunshine/Retna; Janette Beckman/Retna; Howard Barlow/Redferns; David Corio/Retna; Tolca/Sunshine/Retna; Marcia Resnick/Retna; Geoffrey Croft/Retna; Gary Gershoff/Retna; Clemens Rikken/Sunshine/Retna; Jon Erkider/Retna; Dimitrios Kambouris/Retna.

Dick Porter, November 2003, London